POEMS OF
EMILY DICKINSON

Poems of
Emily Dickinson

SELECTED AND EDITED
WITH A COMMENTARY BY
LOUIS UNTERMEYER

AND ILLUSTRATED
WITH DRAWINGS BY
HELEN SEWELL

THE HERITAGE PRESS
NORWALK, CONNECTICUT

The Table of Contents

> NOTE TO THE READER: Following the Editor's Postscript will be found a listing, arranged alphabetically, of those poems which have titles; and also an alphabetic index of the first lines of all of the poems.

The Editor's Introduction

ALTHOUGH SHE WROTE more than fifteen hundred poems—
many of them among the tensest and most poignant ever written
—Emily Dickinson was little more than an unimportant spinster
to her contemporaries, a recluse, a nobody. She was undoubtedly
aware of the sharp originality of her work, but she refused to
think of a publisher and, during her lifetime, only three poems
("A Valentine," "The Snake," and "Success") found their way
into print. She regarded publication as "the auction of the mind,"
and, secretly trying to perfect her daringly unorthodox lines, hid
her writing from all but a few privileged eyes.

For years she has haunted the literary world as a mystery, a
lovelorn legend, a perverse and Puritan ghost. Her scant biography has been variously interpreted and misinterpreted. Since
there were almost no outward "events," biographers allowed
themselves the liberty of substituting fanciful, and sometimes
absurd, speculation for dramatic data. The truth seemed too bare,
too colorless.

Emily Dickinson lived and died in the house in which she was
born and, except for a few small trips, never left it. She luxuri-
ated in anonymity; she was happy at playing a "nobody." The
first poem in the *Second Series* of her posthumously collected
work said it emphatically and scornfully:

> How dreary to be somebody!
> How public, like a frog
> To tell your name the livelong day
> To an admiring bog!

The Amherst in which Emily Dickinson lived was scarcely
"an admiring bog" as far as the poet was concerned. It regarded
her reticence (extreme even for New England), her breathless
little verses which achieved a kind of surreptitious circulation,
and her "eccentricities" with a mixture of curiosity and com-

placent pity. Amherst, Massachusetts, where Emily Dickinson was born, was a rural and somewhat remote community in 1830; her mother's dower had been brought to the town by a team of oxen. Her father was a country lawyer, so much adored by his daughter that some biographers have seen a parallel between him and the harshly possessive father of Elizabeth Barrett Browning. "When father is asleep on the sofa," she said, "the house is full"; and her pictures of the Deity—tributes that are sometimes teasing, sometimes petulant, often irreverent, but always intimate—are all father images.

The first Dickinson to come to New England was born in England in 1600. He was Nathaniel Dickinson and, after trying several communities, to which he apparently could not conform, he moved from Massachusetts to Connecticut and then back again, settling finally in the town of Hadley. Three generations later in 1742, the family was established in the "Third Precinct" of Hadley, which, a little later, became the town of Amherst. Samuel Fowler Dickinson, Emily's grandfather, a deacon, lawyer, and member of the Massachusetts Senate, was one of the prime movers in the founding of Amherst Academy (afterwards Amherst College) and it was his name which headed the list of subscribers. The eldest of his nine children was Emily's father, Edward Dickinson (1803-1874) who, after attending Amherst College and graduating from Yale (for Amherst had not yet received its charter), became a lawyer, a legislator, congressman, and member of the Governor's Council. He married in his mid-twenties. There were three children: William Austin (born April 16, 1829), Emily (born December 10, 1830), and Lavinia (born February 28, 1833).

Emily Dickinson's education was formal without being repressively academic. She attended the district school and, from ten to seventeen, Amherst Academy. She worshipped her teachers and was proficient, though not brilliant, in "the classical course," in history, botany, English, Latin, French, and German. Her early writings were high-spirited and humorous; she was known as the wit of the school. She delighted in whatever was playful, whimsical, and lightly wayward. In 1847 she was a non-conforming student at Mount Holyoke Female Seminary, only a few miles from Amherst. In her eighteenth year she passed examinations in chemistry, rhetoric, geometry, physiology, and astronomy.

It was only in religion that the young Emily Dickinson was decidedly unorthodox. The prevailing mood of the period—and the order of the day at Mount Holyoke Female Seminary—was rigidly pietistic. Emily was unable to learn the conventional attitudes toward sin and salvation; she could not echo the prescribed evangelical phrases. Her companions were quick to repeat sanctimonious platitudes and assume a penitential tone, especially when they had done no wrong. But Emily took the phrases more seriously; she examined them and herself. Words, to her, were weighty, full of significance, not merely rhetorical sounds or pat responses; the word was a thought, a decision, a deed. When the austere Mary Lyon, founder and first principal of the Seminary, insisted that "a young lady should be so educated that she can go as a missionary at a fortnight's notice," and that "fun is a word no young lady should use," Emily rebelled. When Miss Lyon maintained that Christmas was not "merry" but should be observed as a fast day, Emily Dickinson was outraged; she was the one student who stood up and voiced her objection. When Miss Lyon lectured about total depravity, Emily tried to think of herself as depraved. She wrote wryly of her need of "conversion," declared she had "no particular objection to becoming a Christian," and concluded, with mock self-condemnation, "I am one of the bad ones." When she returned home, during the holidays, it was evident that she was fretful and fatigued. In May her brother Austin appeared and took her back to Amherst. When her father decided that one year at Mount Holyoke had been enough, she was half regretful, half relieved. At eighteen she faced the future with a quick and speculative mind in which there was no touch of resignation.

II

Before she was thirty Emily Dickinson knew that her function as a woman would never be fulfilled. In her twenties an event had occurred which made her withdraw from the world. Poetry became not only her solace but the one outlet for her frustration;

it was her confidential diary, and her concealed defeat. Written in secret, kept from all possible readers, it was, paradoxically, her "letter to the world."

At least three sharply differing versions of Emily Dickinson's love story have appeared in print. Up to 1930, the year of her centenary and forty-four years after her death, Emily Dickinson had been pictured as a woman who, after a normal girlhood with its usual quota of beaus, flirtations, and valentines, was suddenly engulfed in a tragic love affair and, realizing its hopelessness, renounced the world, dressed herself in vestal white, and was seen only while flitting about her garden or disappearing around some corner of her darkened house. Between 1930 and 1932 three biographers offered conflicting evidence to support their claims to four different candidates in the role of Emily Dickinson's lover—for it was agreed that her poetry of love and loss was the agonized product of experience rather than overactive imagination. In *The Life and Mind of Emily Dickinson* Genevieve Taggard presented two men who seem to have been involved "in some very vital way with Emily's existence as a poet": Leonard Humphrey, a "beloved teacher" who died when she was twenty, and, later, George Gould, a young man whose prospects were so dim that Emily's father not only frowned on him but forbade his daughter to meet her suitor; whereupon Emily abjured love forever, swore that she "never again would go outside the gate, but live the life of a recluse." In *Emily Dickinson: The Human Background* Josephine Pollitt identified another and far more surprising person as the man who was responsible for the crisis in Emily Dickinson's life and the consequent love poems: Edward Hunt, a dashing but idealistic lieutenant, husband of the author Helen (Jackson) Hunt, who was one of Emily Dickinson's few intimate friends. In *Emily Dickinson Face to Face* Martha Dickinson Bianchi (Emily's niece, the only daughter of Emily's brother Austin and his wife, Emily's "pseudo-sister" Sue) repeated and embroidered the gossip about Emily's abortive affair with an anonymous married clergyman. Mme. Bianchi enlarged upon the hushed legend; in stage whispers she told of Emily's refusal to elope and ruin another woman's happiness, of a sudden wild flight, an ardent pursuit, a violent scene, and a final melodramatic abnegation.

The possibility that Edward Hunt was Emily Dickinson's lost or unattainable love was the theme of a play, *Brittle Heaven* (1934), by Vincent York and Frederick J. Pohl. Another drama, Susan Glaspell's *Alison's House*, was based on the posthumous publication of the poems and was awarded the Pulitzer Prize in 1931. A third play, *Eastward in Eden* by Dorothy Gardner, produced in 1947, centered about a theatricalized version of Emily Dickinson's frustrated love for the Reverend Charles Wadsworth.

The widely contrasting accumulation of Dickinsonia continued to grow. In one year alone (1951) there appeared three volumes of varying interest and value. The first was an extended and, in a large degree, new selection of the poet's prose: *Emily Dickinson's Letters to Doctor and Mrs. Josiah Gilbert Holland.* These letters, crowded with intimate confidences, domestic details, and strays of poetry, are rich in revelations of the life and ways of the period, and furnish fresh evidence of Emily's maturing mind. This was followed by a "shocker": Rebecca Patterson's *The Riddle of Emily Dickinson*. Based upon a mass of misreadings, irrelevant surmises, and a completely false hypothesis, Mrs. Patterson attempted to "prove" that the poet was a Lesbian, and that her poetry was a long and doleful compensation for the loss of a young widow (Kate Scott Turner, Sue's onetime schoolmate) who had paid a few visits to the Dickinson home. Instead of finding Mrs. Patterson's conclusions sensational, the critics agreed that they were as invalid as they were unwarranted. The end of the year produced another biography, Richard Chase's *Emily Dickinson*, a dignified, sensitive, and scholarly, if unexciting, examination of the poet and, more particularly, her writing.

Long before this, in 1938, a book had been published which clarified the "mystery," sifted the tales and conjectures, and established a convincing relation of the woman to her work. In spite of more recent reappraisals, it remains the most authoritative as well as the most readable biography. In *This Was a Poet*, George Frisbie Whicher, himself a poet who had taught at Amherst for a quarter of a century and had examined the facts as well as the legends, traced the outlines of a straightforward and inevitable series of events. It was, Whicher makes plain, the literal truth when Emily Dickinson wrote: "My life has been too simple and stern to embarrass any."

In 1862, when she was thirty-two, Emily Dickinson sent a letter to Thomas Wentworth Higginson, author and critic and "discoverer" of her poetry. In it she showed how close—or how distant—had been the two men who had influenced and affected her most deeply. She wrote: "When a little girl, I had a friend who taught me Immortality; but, venturing too near, himself, he never returned. Soon after my tutor died, and for several years my lexicon was my only companion. Then I found one more, but he was not contented I be his scholar, so he left the land." She said the same thing, but with far greater intensity, in her poetry, notably in the poems beginning "My life closed twice before its close" and "I never lost as much but twice."

Thanks to Whicher, it is no longer hard to brush aside the fog of distorting conjecture and see clearly the two men who meant so much to her: the early friend, the preceptor who died, and the later inspirer who declined to take Emily as his scholar and, leaving her, "left the land." The first was Benjamin Franklin Newton, nine years older than Emily Dickinson and, when she met him, a law student in her father's office. They formed an immediate friendship—he was twenty-seven and she barely eighteen when she wrote to her future sister-in-law "I have found a beautiful new friend!" Unlike Leonard Humphrey, her first teacher, Newton was not a scholar, but he was an ardent reader of unorthodox literature, a thinker at odds with his times. He talked to his young admirer with fire and eloquence not only about the essentials of life but on topics which his contemporaries considered taboo. He wrote revealing letters and sent her books —she was particularly grateful for a copy of Emerson's *Poems*, which provoked new appraisals and helped shape her peculiar style. But she was not in love with Newton nor was he in love with her. Three years after meeting her, Newton married a woman twelve years older than himself. Ill of tuberculosis at the time of his marriage, he died in 1853, a few days after his thirty-second birthday. Emily had grown to regard him not only as her dearest friend and most stimulating mentor, but as an older and wiser brother. Although she knew of his illness, the shock of his dying was profound and his influence was openly acknowledged. Ten months after his death, in a letter asking details of his pastor, she wrote: "Mr. Newton was with my father two years before going to Worcester, in pursuing his studies, and was much in our family. I was then but a child, yet I was old enough to admire the strength, the grace, of an intellect far surpassing my own, and it taught me many lessons, for which I thank it humbly, now that it is gone. Mr. Newton became to me a gentle yet grave Preceptor, teaching me what to read, what authors to admire, what was most grand or beautiful in nature, and that sublime lesson, a faith in things unseen, and in a life again, noble and much more blessed. . . . Of all these things he spoke— he taught of them all, earnestly, tenderly; and when he went from us, it was as an elder brother, loved indeed very much, and mourned and remembered."

This was, undoubtedly, the "friend who taught me Immortality" and who, venturing too near it himself, "never returned." This was the first tragic parting, "mourned and remembered," the first "closing" of her life so poignantly recorded in her verse:

> My life closed twice before its close;
>   It yet remains to see
> If Immortality unveil
>   A third event to me,
> So huge, so hopeless to conceive,
>   As these that twice befell.
> Parting is all we know of heaven,
>   And all we need of hell.

The bitterness of death, the aftermath of loss, and the emptiness of life alone—a life twice about to be richly companioned and twice denied fulfillment—are repeated with renewed pain and an even greater condensation of anguish in the seemingly cryptic but increasingly candid lines:

> I never lost as much but twice,
>   And that was in the sod;
> Twice have I stood a beggar
>   Before the door of God.

> Angels, twice descending,
>   Reimbursed my store.
> Burglar, banker, father,
>   I am poor once more!

But the first loss, sudden and cruel though it must have been, was not crippling. It was the second descent of the angels which, promising to "reimburse" the lonely beggar, left the supplicant at the very door of heaven, rejected and robbed, poorer and lonelier than ever.

A little more than a year after Newton's death, Emily Dickinson took a short trip to visit with her father in Washington. In Philadelphia, in May, 1854, when Emily was midway between twenty-three and twenty-four, she heard a sermon by the Reverend Charles Wadsworth, admired the preacher, and fell in love with him. He was forty, married, pastor of the Arch Street Presbyterian Church, a quiet but devoted servant of God. Contented, modest, and immersed in his work, he was probably unaware of the fervor he had roused in the heart of one of his shyest listeners. But Emily Dickinson knew what had happened to her.

Returning to Amherst, Emily Dickinson brooded on the spell woven by the minister and, unconsciously, by the man. Her hopes for greater intimacy must have been faint, but they persisted. It is likely that some of her poems are largely dramatizations of her secret hopes, fears, and dreams, rather than a record of events; but the breathless anticipation, the deferred delight, and final disappointment are too powerful to be imaginary. It is impossible to draw a dividing line between the wish and the act, the accurate moment and the blurring memory. Besides, the poet warns us:

> The vision, pondered long,
>   So plausible becomes
> That I esteem the fiction real—
>   The real, fictitious seems.

The reality, robbed of visionary magnification, indicates that there were no more than two or three meetings—occasional or chance visits rather than clandestine reunions—and an intermittent correspondence. Nevertheless, Emily's mind was fixed and her heart was pledged. Infatuation grew into obsession; she clung to some hope of companionship with desperate longing. When she learned that the Reverend Wadsworth had received a call to a pulpit in San Francisco, she was filled with terror— "Parting is all we know of heaven/And all we need of hell." She said it explicitly in the poem which begins painfully but calmly:

> I cannot live with you,
> It would be life,
> And life is over there. . . .

and ends brokenly:

> So we must keep apart,
> You there, I here,
> With just the door ajar
> That oceans are,
> And prayer,
> And that pale sustenance,
> Despair!

In retrospect, the poet may have heightened the pitch of grief; the woman compelled by the craftsman may have used the old sorrow as a crying theme rather than a catharsis. But in most of the love poems the anguish is as genuine as it is obvious. It is heard, fiercely but unforced, in such poems as the ones beginning "Dare you see a soul at the white heat?" "Who never lost, are unprepared," "God gave a loaf to every bird, But just a crumb to me," "Of all the souls that stand create," "Pain has an element of blank," "I dreaded that first robin so," "The heart asks pleasure first," "I never lost as much but twice," " 'Twas a long parting," "This merit hath the worst," "At least to pray is left, is left," and the tight-lipped verses entitled "Emancipation."

Equally pathetic is the wish-fulfillment, the unrealized ecstasy, in the stanzas beginning "Our share of night to bear," "I gave myself to him," "Come slowly, Eden!" "I'm wife; I've finished that, that other state," and "Mine by the right of the white election!"

But, although Emily got so she could hear the man's name

without "the stopsensation in my soul" and could open the box which contained his letters "without that forcing in my breath as staples driven through," it was a long time before she could resign herself to a Grace ("I think they call it 'God' ") "renowned to ease extremity." It was not resignation that drove her to make an uneasy peace and forced her to conclude:

> At leisure is the Soul
> That gets a staggering blow;
> The width of Life before it spreads
> Without a thing to do.

Emily Dickinson did not see her "dearest earthly friend," "the fugitive, whom to know was life," for twenty years. She had dedicated herself to him all the time. He returned to Philadelphia and came to see her one day during the summer of 1880. Two years later he was dead, at the age of sixty-nine. Emily survived him by only four years. His picture and a privately printed book of his sermons were found among her most guarded possessions. His death was greater to her than all the other denials. In grief she wrote: "I do not yet fathom that he has died, and hope I may not till he assists me in another world."

She had kept herself to herself ever since she was twenty-five. Now, at fifty-two, she was more than ever alone. She still had a few friends, but she rarely saw them. Her sister Lavinia was a buffer between her and a curious world; she withdrew increasingly into a shell of solitude. She meditated continually on life and eternity, but shunned the church. She loved music but, declining to come in the room where it was played, remained seated outside in the obscurity of the hall. An indefatigable writer, she refused to address the envelopes of her letters. Immuring herself in a peculiar privacy, sending cryptic little verses with gifts of flowers and jellies to wondering neighbors and uncomprehending children, she became the town's prime oddity. Even the appreciative Higginson referred to her as "my partially cracked poetess." In 1883 her health began to fail. She suffered from nervous prostration, although she maintained that "the crisis of the sorrow of so many years is all that tires me." She contracted Bright's disease and died May 15, 1886.

III

The publication of Emily Dickinson's posthumous work is part of a long and confused history. It begins with Lavinia Dickinson, who inherited all the manuscripts—more than 1,800 verses, letters, and fragments—left by her sister. Lavinia was no intellectual. Besides being a zealous housekeeper and a virulent gossip, she was a suspicious guardian of Emily's privacy. But, though she scarcely understood poetry, she "felt" the originality of her sister's gift. After Emily's death, Lavinia did everything she could to justify her sister's withdrawal from the world. As a tribute to her memory—and in the hope of establishing her reputation—she turned for help to a neighbor, Mabel Loomis Todd, who had been close to Emily during the latter part of her life. Mrs. Todd, wife of an Amherst professor of Astronomy, declined to attempt the task alone and enlisted the aid of Colonel Thomas Wentworth Higginson, who had been consulted by Emily and who had been fascinated by her extraordinary images and verbal daring. Together they prepared a selection of some 115 verses which were published as *Poems of Emily Dickinson* in 1890. The title-page declared that the book was "Edited by two of her Friends, Mabel Loomis Todd and Thomas Wentworth Higginson." In 1891, another 167 verses were selected by the same editors and published as *Poems: Second Series*. In 1893 both books were republished in one volume.

Contrary to popular belief, the publication of Emily Dickinson's poetry was not a failure. There was so much interest that Mrs. Todd decided to present some of Emily Dickinson's prose writings, the more so since Emily's correspondence was as sharply characteristic as her verse. A collection entitled *Letters of Emily Dickinson*, edited by Mabel Loomis Todd in two volumes, was published in 1894. It contained almost 100 hitherto unpublished poems, rhymed aphorisms, and scraps of verse. In 1896 another collection of 176 poems was published as *Poems: Third Series*, edited by Mabel Loomis Todd alone.

All of these volumes were somewhat arbitrarily edited. Emily Dickinson had a way of jotting down on the backs of recipes, insides of envelopes, random sheets, brown paper bags from the grocer, and small pieces of paper bound together in "fascicles," several different versions of a stanza and many different choices of words. Sometimes her manuscripts were so crowded with variants that it was impossible to determine what word or words she may have preferred. Her editors had to ignore her indecisions and decide for her. This gave many of Emily Dickinson's printed verses a false finality. In some cases the words were misread, titles (not the poet's, and often misleading) were added, and even rhymes were changed for the sake of smoothness and "euphony." While her work was never so flagrantly "polished" or embellished as Rimsky-Korsakov's alterations of the "roughness" of Mussorgsky, nevertheless all of Emily Dickinson's editors took considerable liberties.

After 1894 there was a silence and a lapse of twenty years before more of Emily Dickinson's unpublished work appeared. Lavinia quarreled with her neighbors, the Todds, over a few feet of disputed land adjoining their properties. In 1896 there was a law suit which involved unpleasant recriminations and brought to light gossip concerning the relations of Emily's late brother, Austin, and the attractive Mrs. Todd. As a result of the suit and the scandal, Mrs. Todd was no longer permitted to publish any of Emily Dickinson's writings, although she remained in possession of many unprinted manuscripts. Upon the death of Lavinia, the estate and all the literary properties went to Emily's niece, Martha Dickinson Bianchi, daughter of Sue and Austin Dickinson. In 1914, a new collection of 143 hitherto unpublished poems, appeared under the title *The Single Hound*, edited by Martha Dickinson Bianchi. After another fifteen years, just a few months before the centenary of the poet's birth, Martha Dickinson Bianchi and a friend, Alfred Leete Hampson, edited and published *Further Poems of Emily Dickinson*, with a tantalizing subtitle: "Withheld from Publication by her Sister Lavinia."

Further Poems was hailed as the most important publishing event of 1929. Although it showed no new aspect of Emily Dickinson's life or genius, it revealed, with renewed sharpness and more detail, delicate contours of her particular world. In spite of faulty punctuation and dubious transliteration, critics found fresh examples of the poet's private blend of grace and profundity. Long before Archibald MacLeish disturbed academicians by insisting that:

> Poetry should not mean
> But be —

Emily Dickinson quietly concluded:

> Beauty is not caused;
> It is.

In 1914 the English poet, Ralph Hodgson, mused that "God loves an idle rainbow no less than laboring seas"; and sometime in the early 1860's Emily was saying:

> The rainbow never tells me
> That gust and storm are by;
> Yet she is more convincing
> Than philosophy.

Nor was the note of poignant resignation lacking. Had Emily Dickinson never written another love poem, her anguish could have been sensed and summarized in a single quatrain from *Further Poems:*

> I took one draught of life,
> I'll tell you what I paid,
> Precisely an existence —
> The market price, they said.

In 1935, fifty years after the poet's death, her niece released another one hundred and thirty poems and poetic fragments. There was no introduction or explanation of the strange and belated publication. The volume was entitled *Unpublished Poems of Emily Dickinson.* The poet's balance of intensity and restraint was again disclosed, and it was again evident that there were many mistakes in the editing; one short poem, for example, reproduced correctly in facsimile, was misread and misprinted.

Meanwhile, a revised and enlarged edition of the *Letters of Emily Dickinson*, edited by Mabel Loomis Todd, the family's first editor, had appeared in 1931. Besides new pages which enriched the old and placed them in perspective, the book contained source material of prime value, including some 150 odd verses, gnomic stanzas, and improvisations in rhyme. The reader is continually arrested by snatches as breath-taking as:

> Truth is as old as God,
> His twin identity—
> And will endure as long as He,
> A co-eternity,
> And perish on the day
> That He is borne away,
> From mansion of the universe,
> A lifeless Deity.

Emily Dickinson's letters talk and sing in the same breath. The prose is always breaking into poetry—or, rather, poetry is the natural completion of her sometimes unnatural prose. Passages read like portions of unrhymed stanzas which are interlarded—or interrupted—by such a verse as:

> Could mortal lip divine
> The undeveloped freight
> Of a delivered syllable,
> 'Twould crumble with the weight!

For no apparent reason except that the poet hoped to communicate something wonderful, the letter-writer breaks off in the midst of a gossipy letter of thanks for some goodies ("sweet remembrances—sweet specifically") with this amazing irrelevance:

> Go slow, my soul, to feed thyself
> Upon his rare approach.
> Go rapid, lest competing death
> Prevail upon the coach.
> Go timid, should his testing eye
> Determine thee amiss.
> Go boldly, for thou paidst the price,
> Redemption for a kiss.

In 1937 there appeared the authoritative and first definitive

Collected Poems, which assembled all those previously brought together by the various editors. It included over 900 poems and was regarded as a landmark in American literature.

Madame Bianchi died in 1943. Mrs. Todd had died in 1932, but she had left more than 650 unpublished poems to her daughter, Millicent Todd Bingham. These poems (many of them among Emily Dickinson's most provocative) appeared in the somewhat startlingly entitled *Bolts of Melody* in 1945, with an illuminating preface by Mabel Loomis Todd, who had helped edit them years before her death, and Millicent Todd Bingham. In the same year Mrs. Bingham issued *Ancestors' Brocades*, which told the story of the Dickinson feud and the subsequent fracas, authenticated by a full account of Lavinia's suspicious dealings, the resulting confusions, fabrications, frauds and law-suits—all of it constituting a record as petty as it was pathetic.

In 1950 Gilbert Holland Montague, of New York, purchased Emily Dickinson's poems, letters, and other papers, and presented the priceless manuscript collection to Harvard University. There had been constant complaints concerning the careless editing and interpretation of the Dickinson writings, and an authentic edition was often demanded. Because of the inaccessibility of the manuscripts, scholars were unable to study the originals and learn how garbled the printed versions may have been. With the great part of her work housed in the Houghton Library it became easier to decipher the mind and true intention of a distorted creative spirit. The task of sorting, arranging, and editing the papers was assigned to Thomas H. Johnson, of Lawrenceville, New Jersey. Besides being an eminent scholar and teacher, Johnson was a skilled researcher who, in 1939, discovered and edited the extraordinary poems of the eighteenth century American "metaphysical," Edward Taylor.

Now that the feud is over, the factions ended, and the possessions in the hands of an impartial custodian, a new text may be forthcoming. Based on a possible chronological order, an exact transcription may bring unity to the scattered parts and reveal the woman's autobiography in the development of the poet's work.

IV

It can never be finally determined how much of Emily Dickinson's poetry is a literal transcript of actual experience and how much is an extension and sublimation of it. In a letter to Colonel Higginson (July, 1862) she declared: "When I state myself as the representative of the verse it does not mean me but a supposed person." There were, it seems, two people at work on the verses which Emily Dickinson wrote and put away: the quietly suffering woman, outliving a crippling disappointment, and "the supposed person" who dramatized her defeat. In *The Bewitched Parsonage* (1950) William Stanley Braithwaite wrote: "Emily is the proof positive that what we call necessary experience pales to insignificance when placed in contrast to inner knowledge. She was a spirit that emerged independent of the material event. . . . Emily's soul was forever innocent, forever completely knowing." Braithwaite was writing about Emily Brontë, but the sentences apply with equal aptness to Emily Dickinson. Nowhere in literature has intuition, that "inner knowledge," so radiantly transcended the fact and surrounded the experience with a beauty which, surpassing the event, makes it immortal.

Immortality is achieved in Emily Dickinson's contradiction of styles, in her unique blend of reticence and flamboyance. She startled her contemporaries and fascinated her followers two generations later with a sharp poetic idiom that was an unrecognized rebuke to the loose rhetoric of her period. Her images flash with true brilliance, not with superficial glitter; her metaphors, which, at first reading, seem extravagant, are surprisingly exact. Surprise was her natural language. Influenced by the American poet she most admired, Ralph Waldo Emerson, she too learned to:

> mount to Paradise
> By the stairway of surprise.

She wrote sometimes under a tragic cloud, sometimes under a dancing star, sometimes as a bereaved woman, sometimes as a happy, irresponsible child. Often, indeed, her writing is too coy for comfort. There is, at times, an embarrassing affectation, a willful naïveté, as though she were determined to be not only a child but a spoiled child—a child who patronizes the universe and is arch with its Creator. But the pertness suddenly turns to pure perception, and the teasing is forgotten in an almost frightening revelation.

Emily Dickinson's way of writing a poem is baffling to the teacher of strict forms. Her poems are not built on a mathematical formula, but on a pattern which resembles that of a kaleidoscope. The verses shift from design to design, from one unexpected arrangement of words to another. No one effect is fixed for long; everything changes, dissolves, and reassembles. Almost any eight lines disclose the waywardness of her figures, the playfulness of her speech and the contradictions of her tone and technique. Her stanzas are composed of curious simplicities of statement followed by swift leaps of insight, at once whimsical and full of wonder. Hers is a style which is both spontaneous and subtle, delicate but durable.

Her themes are few. The instincts of her first editors were not wrong, although their final judgments were arbitrary, when the poems appeared in print, arranged in four convenient categories: Life, Love, Nature, Time and Eternity. Yet, within the limitations of her subject matter—an entire poetry confined to short lyrics—the fusion of observation and imagination is so uncanny as to be beyond ordinary consciousness. It is nothing less than magic that can translate a dog's padding into "belated feet, like intermittent plush," that can see a train, like some catlike monster, "lap the miles, and lick the valleys up," that can watch a storm provoke "a strange mob of panting trees," and observe evening, "the housewife in the west," sweep the sky "with many-colored brooms and leave the shreds behind." Magic it is that condenses tremendous emotional excitement in a phrase like "the silver reticence of death" and "death's stiff stare" or even in a single word—such as the word "accent" in the tense line, "The accent of a coming foot"—or the word "zero" to describe the feeling of horror at encountering a snake: "zero at the bone." Hers is a new poetic vocabulary, dazzling and audacious, in which the homely and the highly imaginative are joined—noon is "the parlor of the day," frost is "the blond assassin," music is "the silver strife," clouds are "listless elephants," shadows "hold their breath," gentlewomen have "dimity convictions," the lightning "skips like mice."

On every page the reader understands the pleasure of the writer; he cannot help but share the delight with which Emily Dickinson manipulated her alternately rich and lean phrases, paired her suspended rhymes, and muted her wry dissonances. Her mind, like her idiom, was so much her own that there is nothing in literature quite like her unpredictable twists of thought, her rapid juxtapositions of the trivial and tremendous, and her trick of changing cryptic non-sequiturs into crystal epigrams. There is no way of measuring her reach or her depth; she is inexhaustible and inimitable.

Here, then, are the songs of one who transmuted the simple lyric into a medium of tremendous power of communication— one who lived in solitude and silence, and became the greatest woman poet ever to write in any language.   L. U.

POEMS: FIRST SERIES

The Editor's Commentary

THE FIRST of the *Poems of Emily Dickinson* was published in November, 1890. It was an unassuming posthumous volume bound in a modest gray cloth that would have pleased the poet who died four years before the book was issued. The selection was made, edited, and, in some instances, "amended" by Emily Dickinson's two friends, Mabel Loomis Todd and Colonel Thomas Wentworth Higginson. Although Mrs. Todd did the major work of deciphering and transcribing the hundreds of small manuscripts, it was Higginson who wrote the Preface:

"The verses of Emily Dickinson belong emphatically to what Emerson long since called 'the Poetry of the Portfolio,'—something produced absolutely without the thought of publication, and solely by way of expression of the writer's own mind. Such verse must inevitably forfeit whatever advantage lies in the discipline of public criticism and the enforced conformity to accepted ways. On the other hand, it may often gain something through the habit of freedom and the unconventional utterance of daring thoughts. In the case of the present author, there was absolutely no choice in the matter; she must write thus, or not at all. A recluse by temperament and habit, literally spending years without setting her foot beyond the doorstep, and many more years during which her walks were strictly limited to her father's grounds, she habitually concealed her mind, like her person, from all but a very few friends; and it was with great difficulty that she was persuaded to print, during her lifetime, three or four poems. Yet she wrote verses in great abundance; and though curiously indifferent to all conventional rules, had yet a rigorous literary standard of her own.

"Miss Dickinson was born in Amherst, Mass., Dec. 10, 1830, and died there May 15, 1886. Her father, Hon. Edward Dickinson, was the leading lawyer of Amherst, and was treasurer of the well-known college there situated. It was his custom once a year to hold a large reception at his house, attended by all the families connected with the institution and by the leading people of the town. On these occasions his daughter Emily emerged from her wonted retirement and did her part as gracious hostess; nor would any one have known from her manner, I have been told, that this was not a daily occurrence. The annual occasion once past, she withdrew again into her seclusion, and except for a very few friends was as invisible to the world as if she had dwelt in a nunnery. For myself, although I had corresponded with her for many years, I saw her but twice face to face, and brought away the impression of something as unique and remote as Undine.

"This selection from her poems is published to meet the desire of her personal friends, and especially of her surviving sister. It is believed that the thoughtful reader will find in these pages a quality more suggestive of the poetry of William Blake than of anything to be elsewhere found,—flashes of wholly original and profound insight into nature and life; words and phrases exhibiting an extraordinary vividness of descriptive and imaginative power, yet often set in a seemingly whimsical or even rugged frame. They are here published as they were written, with very few and superficial changes; although it is fair to say that the titles have been assigned, almost invariably, by the editors. In many cases these verses will seem to the reader like poetry torn up by the roots, with rain and dew and earth still clinging to them, giving a freshness and a fragrance not otherwise to be conveyed. In other cases, as in the few poems of shipwreck or of mental conflict, we can only wonder at the gift of vivid imagination by which this recluse woman can delineate, by a few touches, the very crises of physical or mental struggle. And sometimes again we catch glimpses of a lyric strain, sustained perhaps but for a line or two at a time, and making the reader regret its sudden cessation. But the main quality of these poems is that of extraordinary grasp and insight, uttered with an uneven vigor sometimes exasperating, seemingly wayward, but really unsought and inevitable. After all, when a thought takes one's breath away, a lesson on grammar seems an impertinence. As Ruskin wrote in his earlier and better days, 'No weight nor mass nor beauty of execution can outweigh one grain or fragment.' "

PRELUDE

This is my letter to the world,
    That never wrote to me,—
The simple news that Nature told,
    With tender majesty.

Her message is committed
    To hands I cannot see;
For love of her, sweet countrymen,
    Judge tenderly of me!

I. *Success*

Success is counted sweetest
By those who ne'er succeed.
To comprehend a nectar
Requires sorest need.

Not one of all the purple host
Who took the flag to-day
Can tell the definition,
So clear, of victory,

As he, defeated, dying,
On whose forbidden ear
The distant strains of triumph
Break, agonized and clear.

II

Our share of night to bear,
Our share of morning,
Our blank in bliss to fill,
Our blank in scorning.

Here a star, and there a star,
Some lose their way.
Here a mist, and there a mist,
Afterwards—day!

III. *Rouge et Noir*

Soul, wilt thou toss again?
By just such a hazard
Hundreds have lost, indeed,
But tens have won an all.

Angels' breathless ballot
Lingers to record thee;
Imps in eager caucus
Raffle for my soul.

IV. *Rouge Gagne*

'T is so much joy! 'T is so much joy!
If I should fail, what poverty!
And yet, as poor as I
Have ventured all upon a throw;
Have gained! Yes! Hesitated so
This side the victory!

Life is but life, and death but death!
Bliss is but bliss, and breath but breath!
And if, indeed, I fail,
At least to know the worst is sweet.
Defeat means nothing but defeat,
No drearier can prevail!

And if I gain,—oh, gun at sea,
Oh, bells that in the steeples be,
At first repeat it slow!
For heaven is a different thing
Conjectured, and waked sudden in,
And might o'erwhelm me so!

V

Glee! the great storm is over!
Four have recovered the land;
Forty gone down together
Into the boiling sand.

Ring, for the scant salvation!
Toll, for the bonnie souls,—
Neighbor and friend and bridegroom,
Spinning upon the shoals!

How they will tell the shipwreck
When winter shakes the door,
Till the children ask, "But the forty?
Did they come back no more?"

Then a silence suffuses the story,
And a softness the teller's eye;
And the children no further question,
And only the waves reply.

VI

If I can stop one heart from breaking,
I shall not live in vain;
If I can ease one life the aching,
Or cool one pain,
Or help one fainting robin
Unto his nest again,
I shall not live in vain.

VII. *Almost!*

Within my reach!
I could have touched!
I might have chanced that way!
Soft sauntered through the village,
Sauntered as soft away!
So unsuspected violets
Within the fields lie low,
Too late for striving fingers
That passed, an hour ago.

VIII

A wounded deer leaps highest,
I've heard the hunter tell;
'T is but the ecstasy of death,
And then the brake is still.

The smitten rock that gushes,
The trampled steel that springs:
A cheek is always redder
Just where the hectic stings!

Mirth is the mail of anguish,
In which it caution arm,
Lest anybody spy the blood
And "You're hurt" exclaim!

IX

The heart asks pleasure first,
And then, excuse from pain;
And then, those little anodynes
That deaden suffering;

And then, to go to sleep;
And then, if it should be
The will of its Inquisitor,
The liberty to die.

X. *In a Library*

A precious, mouldering pleasure 't is
To meet an antique book,
In just the dress his century wore;
A privilege, I think,
His venerable hand to take,
And warming in our own,
A passage back, or two, to make
To times when he was young.

His quaint opinions to inspect,
His knowledge to unfold
On what concerns our mutual mind,
The literature of old;
What interested scholars most,
What competitions ran
When Plato was a certainty,
And Sophocles a man;

When Sappho was a living girl,
And Beatrice wore
The gown that Dante deified.
Facts, centuries before,
He traverses familiar,
As one should come to town
And tell you all your dreams were true:
He lived where dreams were sown.

His presence is enchantment,
You beg him not to go;
Old volumes shake their vellum heads
And tantalize, just so.

XI

Much madness is divinest sense
To a discerning eye;
Much sense the starkest madness.
'T is the majority
In this, as all, prevails.
Assent, and you are sane;
Demur,—you're straightway dangerous,
And handled with a chain.

XII

I asked no other thing,
No other was denied.
I offered Being for it;
The mighty merchant smiled.

Brazil? He twirled a button,
Without a glance my way:
"But, madam, is there nothing else
That we can show to-day?"

XIII. *Exclusion*

The soul selects her own society,
Then shuts the door;
On her divine majority
Obtrude no more.

Unmoved, she notes the chariot's pausing
At her low gate;
Unmoved, an emperor is kneeling
Upon her mat.

I've known her from an ample nation
Choose one;
Then close the valves of her attention
Like stone.

XIV. *The Secret*

Some things that fly there be,—
Birds, hours, the bumble-bee:
Of these no elegy.

Some things that stay there be,—
Grief, hills, eternity:
Nor this behooveth me.

There are, that resting, rise.
Can I expound the skies?
How still the riddle lies!

XV. *The Lonely House*

I know some lonely houses off the road
A robber'd like the look of,—
Wooden barred,
And windows hanging low,
Inviting to
A portico,
Where two could creep:
One hand the tools,
The other peep
To make sure all's asleep.
Old-fashioned eyes,
Not easy to surprise!

How orderly the kitchen'd look by night,
With just a clock,—
But they could gag the tick,
And mice won't bark;
And so the walls don't tell,
None will.

A pair of spectacles ajar just stir—
An almanac's aware.
Was it the mat winked,
Or a nervous star?
The moon slides down the stair
To see who's there.

There's plunder,—where?
Tankard, or spoon,
Earring, or stone,
A watch, some ancient brooch

To match the grandmamma,
Staid sleeping there.

    Day rattles, too,
    Stealth's slow;
    The sun has got as far
    As the third sycamore.
    Screams chanticleer,
    "Who's there?"
    And echoes, trains away,
    Sneer—"Where?"
    While the old couple, just astir,
    Fancy the sunrise left the door ajar!

XVI. *Dawn*

When night is almost done,
And sunrise grows so near
That we can touch the spaces,
It's time to smooth the hair

And get the dimples ready,
And wonder we could care
For that old faded midnight
That frightened but an hour.

XVII. *The Mystery of Pain*

Pain has an element of blank;
It cannot recollect
When it began, or if there were
A day when it was not.

It has no future but itself,
Its infinite realms contain
Its past, enlightened to perceive
New periods of pain.

XVIII

I had no time to hate, because
The grave would hinder me,
And life was not so ample I
Could finish enmity.

Nor had I time to love; but since
Some industry must be,
The little toil of love, I thought,
Was large enough for me.

XIX

To fight aloud is very brave,
But gallanter, I know,
Who charge within the bosom,
The cavalry of woe.

Who win, and nations do not see,
Who fall, and none observe,
Whose dying eyes no country
Regards with patriot love.

We trust, in plumed procession,
For such the angels go,
Rank after rank, with even feet
And uniforms of snow.

XX

I taste a liquor never brewed,
From tankards scooped in pearl;
Not all the vats upon the Rhine
Yield such an alcohol!

Inebriate of air am I,
And debauchee of dew,
Reeling, through endless summer days,
From inns of molten blue.

When landlords turn the drunken bee
Out of the foxglove's door,
When butterflies renounce their drams,
I shall but drink the more!

Till seraphs swing their snowy hats,
And saints to windows run,
To see the little tippler
Leaning against the sun!

XXI. *The Book of Martyrs*

Read, sweet, how others strove,
Till we are stouter;
What they renounced,
Till we are less afraid;
How many times they bore
The faithful witness,
Till we are helped,
As if a kingdom cared!

Read then of faith
That shone above the fagot;
Clear strains of hymn
The river could not drown;
Brave names of men
And celestial women,
Passed out of record
Into renown!

XXII. *A Book*

He ate and drank the precious words,
His spirit grew robust;
He knew no more that he was poor,
Nor that his fame was dust.
He danced along the dingy days,
And this bequest of wings
Was but a book. What liberty
A loosened spirit brings!

XXIII. *Unreturning*

'T was such a little, little boat
That toddled down the bay!
'T was such a gallant, gallant sea
That beckoned it away!

'T was such a greedy, greedy wave
That licked it from the coast;
Nor ever guessed the stately sails
My little craft was lost!

XXIV

Whether my bark went down at sea,
Whether she met with gales,
Whether to isles enchanted
She bent her docile sails;

By what mystic mooring
She is held to-day,—
This is the errand of the eye
Out upon the bay.

XXV

Belshazzar had a letter,—
He never had but one;
Belshazzar's correspondent
Concluded and begun
In that immortal copy
The conscience of us all
Can read without its glasses
On revelation's wall.

XXVI

The brain within its groove
Runs evenly and true;
But let a splinter swerve,
'T were easier for you
To put the water back
When floods have slit the hills,
And scooped a turnpike for themselves,
And blotted out the mills!

Poems, First Series: LOVE

I. *Mine*

Mine by the right of the white election!
Mine by the royal seal!
Mine by the sign in the scarlet prison
Bars cannot conceal!

Mine, here in vision and in veto!
Mine, by the grave's repeal
Titled, confirmed,—delirious charter!
Mine, while the ages steal!

II. *Bequest*

You left me, sweet, two legacies,—
A legacy of love
A Heavenly Father would content,
Had He the offer of;

You left me boundaries of pain
Capacious as the sea,
Between eternity and time,
Your consciousness and me.

III

Alter? When the hills do.
Falter? When the sun
Question if his glory
Be the perfect one.

Surfeit? When the daffodil
Doth of the dew:
Even as herself, O friend!
I will of you!

IV. *Suspense*

Elysium is as far as to
The very nearest room,
If in that room a friend await
Felicity or doom.

What fortitude the soul contains,
That it can so endure
The accent of a coming foot,
The opening of a door!

V. *Surrender*

Doubt me, my dim companion!
Why, God would be content
With but a fraction of the love
Poured thee without a stint.
The whole of me, forever,
What more the woman can,—
Say quick, that I may dower thee
With last delight I own!

It cannot be my spirit,
For that was thine before;
I ceded all of dust I knew,—
What opulence the more
Had I, a humble maiden,
Whose farthest of degree
Was that she might,
Some distant heaven,
Dwell timidly with thee!

VI

If you were coming in the fall,
I'd brush the summer by
With half a smile and half a spurn,
As housewives do a fly.

If I could see you in a year,
I'd wind the months in balls,
And put them each in separate drawers,
Until their time befalls.

If only centuries delayed,
I'd count them on my hand,
Subtracting till my fingers dropped
Into Van Diemen's land.

If certain, when this life was out,
That yours and mine should be,
I'd toss it yonder like a rind,
And taste eternity.

But now, all ignorant of the length
Of time's uncertain wing,
It goads me, like the goblin bee,
That will not state its sting.

VII. *With a Flower*

I hide myself within my flower,
That wearing on your breast,
You, unsuspecting, wear me too—
And angels know the rest.

I hide myself within my flower,
That, fading from your vase,
You, unsuspecting, feel for me
Almost a loneliness.

VIII. *Proof*

That I did always love,
I bring thee proof:
That till I loved
I did not love enough.

That I shall love alway,
I offer thee
That love is life,
And life hath immortality.

This, dost thou doubt, sweet?
Then have I
Nothing to show
But Calvary.

IX

Have you got a brook in your little heart,
Where bashful flowers blow,
And blushing birds go down to drink,
And shadows tremble so?

And nobody knows, so still it flows,
That any brook is there;
And yet your little draught of life
Is daily drunken there.

Then look out for the little brook in March,
When the rivers overflow,
And the snows come hurrying from the hills,
And the bridges often go.

And later, in August it may be,
When the meadows parching lie,
Beware, lest this little brook of life
Some burning noon go dry!

X. *Transplanted*

As if some little Arctic flower,
Upon the polar hem,
Went wandering down the latitudes,
Until it puzzled came
To continents of summer,
To firmaments of sun,
To strange, bright crowds of flowers,
And birds of foreign tongue!
I say, as if this little flower
To Eden wandered in—
What then? Why, nothing, only
Your inference therefrom!

XI. *The Outlet*

My river runs to thee:
Blue sea, wilt welcome me?

My river waits reply.
Oh sea, look graciously!

I'll fetch thee brooks
From spotted nooks,—

Say, sea,
Take me!

XII. *In Vain*

I cannot live with you,
It would be life,
And life is over there
Behind the shelf

The sexton keeps the key to,
Putting up
Our life, his porcelain,
Like a cup

Discarded of the housewife,
Quaint or broken;
A newer Sèvres pleases,
Old ones crack.

I could not die with you,
For one must wait
To shut the other's gaze down,
You could not.

And I, could I stand by
And see you freeze,
Without my right of frost,
Death's privilege?

Nor could I rise with you,
Because your face
Would put out Jesus',
That new grace

Glow plain and foreign
On my homesick eye,
Except that you, than he
Shone closer by.

They'd judge us—how?
For you served Heaven, you know,
Or sought to;
I could not,

Because you saturated sight,
And I had no more eyes
For sordid excellence
As Paradise.

And were you lost, I would be,
Though my name
Rang loudest
On the heavenly fame.

And were you saved,
And I condemned to be
Where you were not,
That self were hell to me.

So we must keep apart,
You there, I here,
With just the door ajar
That oceans are,
And prayer,
And that pale sustenance,
Despair!

XIII. *Renunciation*

There came a day at summer's full
Entirely for me;
I thought that such were for the saints,
Where revelations be.

The sun, as common, went abroad,
The flowers, accustomed, blew,
As if no soul the solstice passed
That maketh all things new.
The time was scarce profaned by speech;
The symbol of a word
Was needless, as at sacrament
The wardrobe of our Lord.

Each was to each the sealed church,
Permitted to commune this time,
Lest we too awkward show
At supper of the Lamb.
The hours slid fast, as hours will,
Clutched tight by greedy hands;
So faces on two decks look back,
Bound to opposing lands.

And so, when all the time had failed,
Without external sound,
Each bound the other's crucifix,
We gave no other bond.
Sufficient troth that we shall rise—
Deposed, at length, the grave—
To that new marriage, justified
Through Calvaries of Love!

XIV. *Love's Baptism*

I'm ceded, I've stopped being theirs;
The name they dropped upon my face
With water, in the country church,
Is finished using now,
And they can put it with my dolls,
My childhood, and the string of spools
I've finished threading too.

Baptized before without the choice,
But this time consciously, of grace
Unto supremest name,
Called to my full, the crescent dropped,
Existence's whole arc filled up
With one small diadem.

My second rank, too small the first,
Crowned, crowing on my father's breast,
A half unconscious queen;
But this time, adequate, erect,
With will to choose or to reject,
And I choose—just a throne.

XV. *Resurrection*

'T was a long parting, but the time
For interview had come;
Before the judgment-seat of God,
The last and second time

These fleshless lovers met,
A heaven in a gaze,
A heaven of heavens, the privilege
Of one another's eyes.

No lifetime set on them,
Apparelled as the new
Unborn, except they had beheld,
Born everlasting now.

Was bridal e'er like this?
A paradise, the host,
And cherubim and seraphim
The most familiar guest.

XVI. *Apocalypse*

I'm wife; I've finished that,
That other state;
I'm Czar, I'm woman now:
It's safer so.

How odd the girl's life looks
Behind this soft eclipse!
I think that earth seems so
To those in heaven now.

This being comfort, then
That other kind was pain;
But why compare?
I'm wife! stop there!

XVII. *The Wife*

She rose to his requirement, dropped
The playthings of her life
To take the honorable work
Of woman and of wife.

If aught she missed in her new day
Of amplitude, or awe,
Or first prospective, or the gold
In using wore away,

It lay unmentioned, as the sea
Develops pearl and weed,
But only to himself is known
The fathoms they abide.

XVIII. *Apotheosis*

Come slowly, Eden!
Lips unused to thee,
Bashful, sip thy jasmines,
As the fainting bee,

Reaching late his flower,
Round her chamber hums,
Counts his nectars—enters,
And is lost in balms!

Poems, First Series: NATURE

I. *Why?*

The murmur of a bee
A witchcraft yieldeth me.
If any ask me why,
'T were easier to die
Than tell.

The red upon the hill
Taketh away my will;
If anybody sneer,
Take care, for God is here,
That's all.

The breaking of the day
Addeth to my degree;
If any ask me how,
Artist, who drew me so,
Must tell!

II

New feet within my garden go,
New fingers stir the sod;
A troubadour upon the elm
Betrays the solitude.

New children play upon the green,
New weary sleep below;
And still the pensive spring returns,
And still the punctual snow!

III. *May-Flower*

Pink, small, and punctual,
Aromatic, low,
Covert in April,
Candid in May,

Dear to the moss,
Known by the knoll,
Next to the robin
In every human soul.

Bold little beauty,
Bedecked with thee,
Nature forswears
Antiquity.

IV

Perhaps you'd like to buy a flower?
But I could never sell.
If you would like to borrow
Until the daffodil

Unties her yellow bonnet
Beneath the village door,
Until the bees, from clover rows
Their hock and sherry draw,

Why, I will lend until just then,
But not an hour more!

V

The bee is not afraid of me,
I know the butterfly;
The pretty people in the woods
Receive me cordially.

The brooks laugh louder when I come,
The breezes madder play.
Wherefore, mine eyes, thy silver mists?
Wherefore, O summer's day?

VI. *A Service of Song*

Some keep the Sabbath going to church;
I keep it staying at home,
With a bobolink for a chorister,
And an orchard for a dome.

Some keep the Sabbath in surplice;
I just wear my wings,
And instead of tolling the bell for church,
Our little sexton sings.

God preaches,—a noted clergyman,—
And the sermon is never long;
So instead of getting to heaven at last,
I'm going all along!

VII. *Summer's Armies*

Some rainbow coming from the fair!
Some vision of the world Cashmere
I confidently see!
Or else a peacock's purple train,
Feather by feather, on the plain
Fritters itself away!

The dreamy butterflies bestir,
Lethargic pools resume the whir
Of last year's sundered tune.
From some old fortress on the sun
Baronial bees march, one by one,
In murmuring platoon!

The robins stand as thick to-day
As flakes of snow stood yesterday,
On fence and roof and twig.
The orchis binds her feather on
For her old lover, Don the Sun,
Revisiting the bog!

Without commander, countless, still,
The regiment of wood and hill
In bright detachment stand.
Behold! Whose multitudes are these?
The children of whose turbaned seas,
Or what Circassian land?

VIII. *The Grass*

The grass so little has to do,—
A sphere of simple green,
With only butterflies to brood,
And bees to entertain,

And stir all day to pretty tunes
The breezes fetch along,
And hold the sunshine in its lap
And bow to everything;

And thread the dews all night, like pearls,
And make itself so fine,—
A duchess were too common
For such a noticing.

And even when it dies, to pass
In odors so divine,
As lowly spices gone to sleep,
Or amulets of pine.

And then to dwell in sovereign barns,
And dream the days away,—
The grass so little has to do,
I wish I were a hay!

IX. *Summer Shower*

A drop fell on the apple tree,
Another on the roof;
A half a dozen kissed the eaves,
And made the gables laugh.

A few went out to help the brook,
That went to help the sea.
Myself conjectured, Were they pearls,
What necklaces could be!

The dust replaced in hoisted roads,
The birds jocoser sung;
The sunshine threw his hat away,
The orchards spangles hung.

The breezes brought dejected lutes,
And bathed them in the glee;
The East put out a single flag,
And signed the fête away.

X

The pedigree of honey
Does not concern the bee;
A clover, any time, to him
Is aristocracy.

XI. *Psalm of the Day*

A something in a summer's day,
As slow her flambeaux burn away,
Which solemnizes me.

A something in a summer's noon,—
An azure depth, a wordless tune,
Transcending ecstasy.

And still within a summer's night
A something so transporting bright,
I clap my hands to see;

Then veil my too inspecting face,
Lest such a subtle, shimmering grace
Flutter too far for me.

The wizard-fingers never rest,
The purple brook within the breast
Still chafes its narrow bed;

Still rears the East her amber flag,
Guides still the sun along the crag
His caravan of red,

Like flowers that heard the tale of dews,
But never deemed the dripping prize
Awaited their low brows;

Or bees, that thought the summer's name
Some rumor of delirium
No summer could for them;

Or Arctic creature, dimly stirred
By tropic hint,—some travelled bird
Imported to the wood;

Or wind's bright signal to the ear,
Making that homely and severe,
Contented, known, before

The heaven unexpected came,
To lives that thought their worshipping
A too presumptuous psalm.

XII. *The Sea of Sunset*

This is the land the sunset washes,
These are the banks of the Yellow Sea;
Where it rose, or whither it rushes,
These are the western mystery!

Night after night her purple traffic
Strews the landing with opal bales;
Merchantmen poise upon horizons,
Dip, and vanish with fairy sails.

XIII

A little road not made of man,
Enabled of the eye,
Accessible to thill of bee,
Or cart of butterfly.

If town it have, beyond itself,
'T is that I cannot say;
I only sigh,—no vehicle
Bears me along that way.

XIV

So bashful when I spied her,
So pretty, so ashamed!
So hidden in her leaflets,
Lest anybody find;

So breathless till I passed her,
So helpless when I turned
And bore her, struggling, blushing,
Her simple haunts beyond!

For whom I robbed the dingle,
For whom betrayed the dell,
Many will doubtless ask me,
But I shall never tell!

XV. *Purple Clover*

There is a flower that bees prefer,
And butterflies desire;
To gain the purple democrat
The humming-birds aspire.

And whatsoever insect pass,
A honey bears away
Proportioned to his several dearth
And her capacity.

Her face is rounder than the moon,
And ruddier than the gown
Of orchis in the pasture,
Or rhododendron worn.

She doth not wait for June;
Before the world is green
Her sturdy little countenance
Against the wind is seen,

Contending with the grass,
Near kinsman to herself,
For privilege of sod and sun,
Sweet litigants for life.

And when the hills are full,
And newer fashions blow,
Doth not retract a single spice
For pang of jealousy.

Her public is the noon,
Her providence the sun,
Her progress by the bee proclaimed
In sovereign, swerveless tune.

The bravest of the host,
Surrendering the last,
Nor even of defeat aware
When cancelled by the frost.

XVI. *The Bee*

Like trains of cars on tracks of plush
I hear the level bee:
A jar across the flowers goes,
Their velvet masonry

Withstands until the sweet assault
Their chivalry consumes,
While he, victorious, tilts away
To vanquish other blooms.

His feet are shod with gauze,
His helmet is of gold;
His breast, a single onyx
With chrysoprase, inlaid.

His labor is a chant,
His idleness a tune;
Oh, for a bee's experience
Of clovers and of noon!

XVII

As children bid the guest good-night,
And then reluctant turn,
My flowers raise their pretty lips,
Then put their nightgowns on.

As children caper when they wake,
Merry that it is morn,
My flowers from a hundred cribs
Will peep, and prance again.

XVIII

Angels in the early morning
May be seen the dews among,
Stooping, plucking, smiling, flying:
Do the buds to them belong?

Angels when the sun is hottest
May be seen the sands among,
Stooping, plucking, sighing, flying;
Parched the flowers they bear along.

XIX. *A Day*

I'll tell you how the sun rose,—
A ribbon at a time.
The steeples swarm in amethyst,
The news like squirrels ran.

The hills untied their bonnets,
The bobolinks begun.
Then I said softly to myself,
"That must have been the sun!"

.   .   .   .   .   .

But how he set, I know not.
There seemed a purple stile
Which little yellow boys and girls
Were climbing all the while

Till when they reached the other side,
A dominie in gray
Put gently up the evening bars,
And led the flock away.

XX

Presentiment is that long shadow on the lawn
Indicative that suns go down;
The notice to the startled grass
That darkness is about to pass.

XXI. *Two Worlds*

It makes no difference abroad,
The seasons fit the same,
The mornings blossom into noons,
And split their pods of flame.

Wild-flowers kindle in the woods,
The brooks brag all the day;
No blackbird bates his jargoning
For passing Calvary.

Auto-da-fé and judgment
Are nothing to the bee;
His separation from his rose
To him seems misery.

XXII. *The Mountain*

The mountain sat upon the plain
In his eternal chair,
His observation omnifold,
His inquest everywhere.

The seasons prayed around his knees,
Like children round a sire:
Grandfather of the days is he,
Of dawn the ancestor.

XXIII. *Death and Life*

Apparently with no surprise
To any happy flower,
The frost beheads it at its play
In accidental power.
The blond assassin passes on,
The sun proceeds unmoved
To measure off another day
For an approving God.

XXIV

'T was later when the summer went
Than when the cricket came,
And yet we knew that gentle clock
Meant nought but going home.

'T was sooner when the cricket went
Than when the winter came,
Yet that pathetic pendulum
Keeps esoteric time.

XXV

The butterfly's assumption-gown,
In chrysoprase apartments hung,
  This afternoon put on.

How condescending to descend,
And be of buttercups the friend
  In a New England town!

XXVI. *The Wind*

Of all the sounds despatched abroad,
There's not a charge to me
Like that old measure in the boughs,
That phraseless melody

The wind does, working like a hand
Whose fingers brush the sky,
Then quiver down, with tufts of tune
Permitted gods and me.

When winds go round and round in bands,
And thrum upon the door,
And birds take places overhead,
To bear them orchestra,

I crave him grace, of summer boughs,
If such an outcast be,
He never heard that fleshless chant
Rise solemn in the tree,

As if some caravan of sound
On deserts, in the sky,
Had broken rank,
Then knit, and passed
In seamless company.

XXVII. *Autumn*

The morns are meeker than they were,
The nuts are getting brown;
The berry's cheek is plumper,
The rose is out of town.

The maple wears a gayer scarf,
The field a scarlet gown.
Lest I should be old-fashioned,
I'll put a trinket on.

XXVIII. *Beclouded*

The sky is low, the clouds are mean,
A travelling flake of snow
Across a barn or through a rut
Debates if it will go.

A narrow wind complains all day
How some one treated him;
Nature, like us, is sometimes caught
Without her diadem.

XXIX. *The Hemlock*

I think the hemlock likes to stand
Upon a marge of snow;
It suits his own austerity,
And satisfies an awe

That men must slake in wilderness,
Or in the desert cloy,—
An instinct for the hoar, the bald,
Lapland's necessity.

The hemlock's nature thrives on cold;
The gnash of northern winds
Is sweetest nutriment to him,
His best Norwegian wines.

To satin races he is nought;
But children on the Don
Beneath his tabernacles play,
And Dnieper wrestlers run.

XXX. *Indian Summer*

These are the days when birds come back,
A very few, a bird or two,
To take a backward look.

These are the days when skies put on
The old, old sophistries of June,—
A blue and gold mistake.

Oh, fraud that cannot cheat the bee,
Almost thy plausibility
Induces my belief,

Till ranks of seeds their witness bear,
And softly through the altered air
Hurries a timid leaf!

Oh, sacrament of summer days,
Oh, last communion in the haze,
Permit a child to join,

Thy sacred emblems to partake,
Thy consecrated bread to break,
Taste thine immortal wine!

XXXI

There's a certain slant of light,
On winter afternoons,
That oppresses, like the weight
Of cathedral tunes.

Heavenly hurt it gives us;
We can find no scar,
But internal difference
Where the meanings are.

None may teach it anything,
'T is the seal, despair,—
An imperial affliction
Sent us of the air.

When it comes, the landscape listens,
Shadows hold their breath;
When it goes, 't is like the distance
On the look of death.

Poems, First Series: TIME AND ETERNITY

I

One dignity delays for all,
One mitred afternoon.
None can avoid this purple,
None evade this crown.

Coach it insures, and footmen,
Chamber and state and throng;
Bells, also, in the village,
As we ride grand along.

What dignified attendants,
What service when we pause!
How loyally at parting
Their hundred hats they raise!

How pomp surpassing ermine,
When simple you and I
Present our meek escutcheon,
And claim the rank to die!

II. *Too Late*

Delayed till she had ceased to know,
Delayed till in its vest of snow
   Her loving bosom lay.
An hour behind the fleeting breath,
Later by just an hour than death,—
   Oh, lagging yesterday!

Could she have guessed that it would be;
Could but a crier of the glee
   Have climbed the distant hill;
Had not the bliss so slow a pace,—
Who knows but this surrendered face
   Were undefeated still?

Oh, if there may departing be
Any forgot by victory
   In her imperial round,
Show them this meek apparelled thing,
That could not stop to be a king,
   Doubtful if it be crowned!

III. *Astra Castra*

Departed to the judgment,
A mighty afternoon;
Great clouds like ushers leaning,
Creation looking on.

The flesh surrendered, cancelled,
The bodiless begun;
Two worlds, like audiences, disperse
And leave the soul alone.

IV

Safe in their alabaster chambers,
Untouched by morning and untouched by noon,
Sleep the meek members of the resurrection,
Rafter of satin, and roof of stone.

Light laughs the breeze in her castle of sunshine;
Babbles the bee in a stolid ear;
Pipe the sweet birds in ignorant cadence,—
Ah, what sagacity perished here!

Grand go the years in the crescent above them;
Worlds scoop their arcs, and firmaments row,
Diadems drop and Doges surrender,
Soundless as dots on a disk of snow.

V

On this long storm the rainbow rose,
On this late morn the sun;
The clouds, like listless elephants,
Horizons straggled down.

The birds rose smiling in their nests,
The gales indeed were done;
Alas! how heedless were the eyes
On whom the summer shone!

The quiet nonchalance of death
No daybreak can bestir;
The slow archangel's syllables
Must awaken her.

VI. *From the Chrysalis*

My cocoon tightens, colors tease,
I'm feeling for the air;
A dim capacity for wings
Degrades the dress I wear.

A power of butterfly must be
The aptitude to fly,
Meadows of majesty concedes
And easy sweeps of sky.

So I must baffle at the hint
And cipher at the sign,
And make much blunder, if at last
I take the clew divine.

VII. *Setting Sail*

Exultation is the going
Of an island soul to sea,—
Past the houses, past the headlands,
Into deep eternity!

Bred as we, among the mountains,
Can the sailor understand
The divine intoxication
Of the first league out from land?

VIII

Look back on time with kindly eyes,
He doubtless did his best;
How softly sinks his trembling sun
In human nature's west!

IX

A train went through a burial gate,
A bird broke forth and sang,
And trilled, and quivered, and shook his throat
Till all the churchyard rang;

And then adjusted his little notes,
And bowed and sang again.
Doubtless, he thought it meet of him
To say good-by to men.

X

I died for beauty, but was scarce
Adjusted in the tomb,
When one who died for truth was lain
In an adjoining room.

He questioned softly why I failed?
"For beauty," I replied.
"And I for truth,—the two are one;
We brethren are," he said.

And so, as kinsmen met a night,
We talked between the rooms,
Until the moss had reached our lips,
And covered up our names.

XI. *"Troubled About Many Things"*

How many times these low feet staggered,
Only the soldered mouth can tell;
Try! can you stir the awful rivet?
Try! can you lift the hasps of steel?

Stroke the cool forehead, hot so often,
Lift, if you can, the listless hair;
Handle the adamantine fingers
Never a thimble more shall wear.

Buzz the dull flies on the chamber window;
Brave shines the sun through the freckled pane;
Fearless the cobweb swings from the ceiling—
Indolent housewife, in daisies lain!

XII. *Real*

I like a look of agony,
Because I know it's true;
Men do not sham convulsion,
Nor simulate a throe.

The eyes glaze once, and that is death.
Impossible to feign
The beads upon the forehead
By homely anguish strung.

XIII. *The Funeral*

That short, potential stir
That each can make but once,
That bustle so illustrious
'T is almost consequence,

Is the *éclat* of death.
Oh, thou unknown renown
That not a beggar would accept,
Had he the power to spurn!

XIV

I went to thank her,
But she slept;
Her bed a funnelled stone,
With nosegays at the head and foot,
That travellers had thrown,

Who went to thank her;
But she slept.
'T was short to cross the sea
To look upon her like, alive,
But turning back 't was slow.

XV

I've seen a dying eye
Run round and round a room
In search of something, as it seemed,
Then cloudier become;
And then, obscure with fog,
And then be soldered down
Without disclosing what it be,
'T were blessed to have seen.

XVI. *Refuge*

The clouds their backs together laid,
The north begun to push,
The forests galloped till they fell,
The lightning skipped like mice;
The thunder crumbled like a stuff—
How good to be safe in tombs,
Where nature's temper cannot reach,
Nor vengeance ever comes!

XVII

I never saw a moor,
I never saw the sea;
Yet know I how the heather looks,
And what a wave must be.

I never spoke with God,
Nor visited in heaven;
Yet certain am I of the spot
As if the chart were given.

XVIII

To know just how he suffered would be dear;
To know if any human eyes were near
To whom he could intrust his wavering gaze,
Until it settled firm on Paradise.

To know if he was patient, part content,
Was dying as he thought, or different;
Was it a pleasant day to die,
And did the sunshine face his way?

What was his furthest mind, of home, or God,
Or what the distant say
At news that he ceased human nature
On such a day?

And wishes, had he any?
Just his sigh, accented,
Had been legible to me.
And was he confident until
Ill fluttered out in everlasting well?

And if he spoke, what name was best,
What first,
What one broke off with
At the drowsiest?

Was he afraid, or tranquil?
Might he know
How conscious consciousness could grow,
Till love that was, and love too blest to be,
Meet—and the junction be Eternity?

XIX

The last night that she lived,
It was a common night,
Except the dying; this to us
Made nature different.

We noticed smallest things,—
Things overlooked before,
By this great light upon our minds
Italicized, as 't were.

That others could exist
While she must finish quite,
A jealousy for her arose
So nearly infinite.

We waited while she passed;
It was a narrow time,
Too jostled were our souls to speak,
At length the notice came.

She mentioned, and forgot;
Then lightly as a reed
Bent to the water, shivered scarce,
Consented, and was dead.

And we, we placed the hair,
And drew the head erect;
And then an awful leisure was,
Our faith to regulate.

XX. *The First Lesson*

Not in this world to see his face
Sounds long, until I read the place
Where this is said to be
But just the primer to a life
Unopened, rare, upon the shelf,
Clasped yet to him and me.

And yet, my primer suits me so
I would not choose a book to know
Than that, be sweeter wise;
Might some one else so learned be,
And leave me just my A B C,
Himself could have the skies.

XXI. *Playmates*

God permits industrious angels
Afternoons to play.
I met one,—forgot my school-mates,
All, for him, straightway.

God calls home the angels promptly
At the setting sun;
I missed mine. How dreary marbles,
After playing Crown!

XXII

The bustle in a house
The morning after death
Is solemnest of industries
Enacted upon earth,—

The sweeping up the heart,
And putting love away
We shall not want to use again
Until eternity.

XXIII

I reason, earth is short,
And anguish absolute.
And many hurt;
But what of that?

I reason, we could die:
The best vitality
Cannot excel decay;
But what of that?

I reason that in heaven
Somehow, it will be even,
Some new equation given;
But what of that?

XXIV

Afraid? Of whom am I afraid?
Not death; for who is he?
The porter of my father's lodge
As much abasheth me.

Of life? 'T were odd I fear a thing
That comprehendeth me
In one or more existences
At Deity's decree.

Of resurrection? Is the east
Afraid to trust the morn
With her fastidious forehead?
As soon impeach my crown!

XXV

Two swimmers wrestled on the spar
Until the morning sun,
When one turned smiling to the land.
O God, the other one!

The stray ships passing spied a face
Upon the waters borne,
With eyes in death still begging raised,
And hands beseeching thrown.

XXVI. *Dying*

The sun kept setting, setting still;
No hue of afternoon
Upon the village I perceived,—
From house to house 't was noon.

The dusk kept dropping, dropping still;
No dew upon the grass,
But only on my forehead stopped,
And wandered in my face.

My feet kept drowsing, drowsing still,
My fingers were awake;
Yet why so little sound myself
Unto my seeming make?

How well I knew the light before!
I could not see it now.
'T is dying, I am doing; but
I'm not afraid to know.

XXVII. *The Chariot*

Because I could not stop for Death,
He kindly stopped for me;
The carriage held but just ourselves
And Immortality.

We slowly drove, he knew no haste,
And I had put away
My labor, and my leisure too,
For his civility.

We passed the school where children played,
Their lessons scarcely done;
We passed the fields of gazing grain,
We passed the setting sun.

We paused before a house that seemed
A swelling of the ground;
The roof was scarcely visible,
The cornice but a mound.

Since then 't is centuries; but each
Feels shorter than the day
I first surmised the horses' heads
Were toward eternity.

XXVIII

She went as quiet as the dew
From a familiar flower.
Not like the dew did she return
At the accustomed hour!

She dropt as softly as a star
From out my summer's eve;
Less skilful than Leverrier
It's sorer to believe!

XXIX. *Resurgam*

At last to be identified!
At last, the lamps upon thy side,
The rest of life to see!
Past midnight, past the morning star!
Past sunrise! Ah! what leagues there are
Between our feet and day!

XXX

Except to heaven, she is nought;
Except for angels, lone;
Except to some wide-wandering bee,
A flower superfluous blown;

Except for winds, provincial;
Except by butterflies,
Unnoticed as a single dew
That on the acre lies.

The smallest housewife in the grass,
Yet take her from the lawn,
And somebody has lost the face
That made existence home!

XXXI

I never lost as much but twice,
And that was in the sod;
Twice have I stood a beggar
Before the door of God.

Angels, twice descending,
Reimbursed my store.
Burglar, banker, father,
I am poor once more!

XXXII

Death is a dialogue between
The spirit and the dust.
"Dissolve," says Death. The Spirit, "Sir,
I have another trust."

Death doubts it, argues from the ground.
The Spirit turns away,
Just laying off, for evidence,
An overcoat of clay.

XXXIII

It was too late for man,
But early yet for God;
Creation impotent to help,
But prayer remained our side.

How excellent the heaven,
When earth cannot be had;
How hospitable, then, the face
Of our old neighbor, God!

XXXIV. *Along the Potomac*

When I was small, a woman died.
To-day her only boy
Went up from the Potomac,
His face all victory,

To look at her; how slowly
The seasons must have turned
Till bullets clipt an angle,
And he passed quickly round!

If pride shall be in Paradise
I never can decide;
Of their imperial conduct,
No person testified.

But proud in apparition,
That woman and her boy
Pass back and forth before my brain,
As ever in the sky.

XXXV

The daisy follows soft the sun,
And when his golden walk is done,
   Sits shyly at his feet.
He, waking, finds the flower near.
"Wherefore, marauder, art thou here?"
   "Because, sir, love is sweet!"

We are the flower, Thou the sun!
Forgive us, if as days decline,
   We nearer steal to Thee,—
Enamoured of the parting west,
The peace, the flight, the amethyst,
   Night's possibility!

XXXVI

I shall know why, when time is over,
And I have ceased to wonder why;
Christ will explain each separate anguish
In the fair schoolroom of the sky.

He will tell me what Peter promised,
And I, for wonder at his woe,
I shall forget the drop of anguish
That scalds me now, that scalds me now.

XXXVII. *Emancipation*

No rack can torture me,
My soul's at liberty.
Behind this mortal bone
There knits a bolder one

You cannot prick with saw,
Nor rend with scymitar.
Two bodies therefore be;
Bind one, and one will flee.

The eagle of his nest
No easier divest
And gain the sky,
Than mayest thou,

Except thyself may be
Thine enemy;
Captivity is consciousness,
So's liberty.

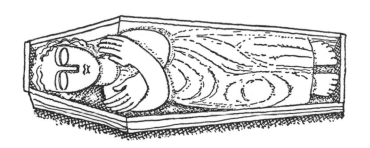

XXXIX

If I should n't be alive
When the robins come,
Give the one in red cravat
A memorial crumb.

If I could n't thank you,
Being just asleep,
You will know I'm trying
With my granite lip!

XXXVIII. *Lost*

I lost a world the other day.
Has anybody found?
You'll know it by the row of stars
Around its forehead bound.

A rich man might not notice it;
Yet to my frugal eye
Of more esteem than ducats.
Oh, find it, sir, for me!

XL

Sleep is supposed to be,
By souls of sanity,
The shutting of the eye.
Sleep is the station grand
Down which on either hand
The hosts of witness stand!

Morn is supposed to be,
By people of degree,
The breaking of the day.

Morning has not occurred!
That shall aurora be
East of eternity;
One with the banner gay,
One in the red array,—
That is the break of day.

POEMS: SECOND SERIES

The Editor's Commentary

Poems of Emily Dickinson: Second Series (1891) followed the first volume in less than a year. Readers of the first collection—and, contrary to legend, there were more than a Gideon's band of readers—wanted more of the epigrammatic phrases and tart rhymes with which the poet put her indubitable mark on every line she wrote. As before, Colonel Higginson aided in the selection and arrangement, and helped determine the final versions. This time, however, the Preface was written by his co-editor, Mabel Loomis Todd, as follows:

"The eagerness with which the first volume of Emily Dickinson's poems has been read shows very clearly that all our alleged modern artificiality does not prevent a prompt appreciation of the qualities of directness and simplicity in approaching the greatest themes,—life and love and death. That 'irresistible needle-touch,' as one of her best critics has called it, piercing at once the very core of a thought, has found a response as wide and sympathetic as it has been unexpected even to those who knew best her compelling power. This second volume, while open to the same criticism as to form with its predecessor, shows also the same shining beauties.

Although Emily Dickinson had been in the habit of sending occasional poems to friends and correspondents, the full extent of her writing was by no means imagined by them. Her friend 'H. H.'* must at least have suspected it, for in a letter dated 5th September, 1884, she wrote:—

MY DEAR FRIEND,—What portfolios full of verses you must have! It is a cruel wrong to your 'day and generation' that you will not give them light.

If such a thing should happen as that I should outlive you, I wish you would make me your literary legatee and executor. Surely after you are what is called "dead" you will be willing that the poor ghosts you have left behind should be cheered and

*Helen Hunt (Jackson), author of *Ramona.*

pleased by your verses, will you not? You ought to be. I do not think we have a right to withhold from the world a word or a thought any more than a *deed* which might help a single soul. . . .

Truly yours,

HELEN JACKSON.

The 'portfolios' were found, shortly after Emily Dickinson's death, by her sister and only surviving housemate. Most of the poems had been carefully copied on sheets of note-paper, and tied in little fascicules, each of six or eight sheets. While many of them bear evidence of having been thrown off at white heat, still more had received thoughtful revision. There is the frequent addition of rather perplexing foot-notes, affording large choice of words and phrases. And in the copies which she sent to friends, sometimes one form, sometimes another, is found to have been used. Without important exception, her friends have generously placed at the disposal of the Editors any poems they had received from her; and these have given the obvious advantage of comparison among several renderings of the same verse.

To what further rigorous pruning her verses would have been subjected had she published them herself, we cannot know. They should be regarded in many cases as merely the first strong and suggestive sketches of an artist, intended to be embodied at some time in the finished picture.

Emily Dickinson appears to have written her first poems in the winter of 1862. In a letter to one of the present Editors the April following, she says, 'I made no verse, but one or two, until this winter.'

The handwriting was at first somewhat like the delicate, running Italian hand of our elder gentlewomen; but as she advanced in breadth of thought, it grew bolder and more abrupt, until in her latest years each letter stood distinct and separate from its fellows. In most of her poems, particularly the later ones, everything by way of punctuation was discarded, except numerous dashes; and all important words began with capitals. The effect of a page of her more recent manuscript is exceedingly quaint and strong. The fac-simile given in the present volume is from one of the earlier transition periods. Although there is nowhere a date, the handwriting makes it possible to arrange the poems with general chronologic accuracy.

As a rule, the verses were without titles; but 'A Country Burial,' 'A Thunder-Storm,' 'The Humming-Bird,' and a few others were named by their author, frequently at the end,—sometimes only in the accompanying note, if sent to a friend.

The variation of readings, with the fact that she often wrote in pencil and not always clearly, have at times thrown a good deal of responsibility upon her Editors. But all interference not absolutely inevitable has been avoided. The very roughness of her own rendering is part of herself, and not lightly to be touched; for it seems in many cases that she intentionally avoided the smoother and more usual rhymes.

Like impressionist pictures, or Wagner's rugged music, the very absence of conventional form challenges attention. In Emily Dickinson's exacting hands, the especial, intrinsic fitness of a particular order of words might not be sacrificed to anything virtually extrinsic; and her verses all show a strange cadence of inner rhythmical music. Lines are always daringly constructed, and the 'thought-rhyme' appears frequently,—appealing, indeed, to an unrecognized sense more elusive than hearing.

Emily Dickinson scrutinized everything with clear-eyed frankness. Every subject was proper ground for legitimate study, even the sombre facts of death and burial, and the unknown life beyond. She touches these themes sometimes lightly, sometimes almost humorously, more often with peculiar power. . . .

She had tried society and the world, and found them lacking. She was not an invalid, and she lived in seclusion from no love-disappointment. Her life was the normal blossoming of a nature introspective to a high degree, whose best thought could not exist in pretence.

Storm, wind, the wild March sky, sunsets and dawns; the birds, and bees, butterflies and flowers of her garden, with a few trusted human friends, were sufficient companionship. The coming of the first robin was a jubilee beyond crowning of monarch or birthday of pope; the first red leaf hurrying through 'the altered air,' an epoch. Immortality was close about her; and while never morbid or melancholy, she lived in its presence."

Prelude: MY NOSEGAYS

My nosegays are for captives;
　Dim, long-expectant eyes,
Fingers denied the plucking,
　Patient till paradise.

To such, if they should whisper
　Of morning and the moor,
They bear no other errand,
　And I, no other prayer.

I

I'm nobody! Who are you?
Are you nobody, too?
Then there's a pair of us—don't tell!
They'd banish us, you know.

How dreary to be somebody!
How public, like a frog
To tell your name the livelong day
To an admiring bog!

II

I bring an unaccustomed wine
To lips long parching, next to mine,
And summon them to drink.

Crackling with fever, they essay;
I turn my brimming eyes away,
And come next hour to look.

The hands still hug the tardy glass;
The lips I would have cooled, alas!
Are so superfluous cold,

I would as soon attempt to warm
The bosoms where the frost has lain
Ages beneath the mould.

Some other thirsty there may be
To whom this would have pointed me
Had it remained to speak.

And so I always bear the cup
If, haply, mine may be the drop
Some pilgrim thirst to slake,—

If, haply, any say to me,
"Unto the little, unto me,"
When I at last awake.

III

The nearest dream recedes, unrealized.
The heaven we chase
Like the June bee
Before the school-boy
Invites the race;
Stoops to an easy clover—
Dips—evades—teases—deploys;
Then to the royal clouds
Lifts his light pinnace
Heedless of the boy
Staring, bewildered, at the mocking sky.

Homesick for steadfast honey,
Ah! the bee flies not
That brews that rare variety.

IV

We play at paste,
Till qualified for pearl,
Then drop the paste,
And deem ourself a fool.
The shapes, though, were similar,
And our new hands
Learned gem-tactics
Practising sands.

V

I found the phrase to every thought
I ever had, but one;
And that defies me,—as a hand
Did try to chalk the sun

To races nurtured in the dark;—
How would your own begin?
Can blaze be done in cochineal,
Or noon in mazarin?

VI. *Hope*

Hope is the thing with feathers
That perches in the soul,
And sings the tune without the words,
And never stops at all,

And sweetest in the gale is heard;
And sore must be the storm
That could abash the little bird
That kept so many warm.

I've heard it in the chillest land,
And on the strangest sea;
Yet, never, in extremity,
It asked a crumb of me.

VII. *The White Heat*

Dare you see a soul at the white heat?
  Then crouch within the door.
Red is the fire's common tint;
  But when the vivid ore

Has sated flame's conditions,
  Its quivering substance plays
Without a color but the light
  Of unanointed blaze.

Least village boasts its blacksmith,
  Whose anvil's even din
Stands symbol for the finer forge
  That soundless tugs within,

Refining these impatient ores
  With hammer and with blaze,
Until the designated light
  Repudiate the forge.

VIII. *Triumphant*

Who never lost, are unprepared
A coronet to find;
Who never thirsted, flagons
And cooling tamarind.

Who never climbed the weary league—
Can such a foot explore
The purple territories
On Pizarro's shore?

How many legions overcome?
The emperor will say.
How many colors taken
On Revolution Day?

How many bullets bearest?
The royal scar hast thou?
Angels, write "Promoted"
On this soldier's brow!

IX. *The Test*

I can wade grief,
Whole pools of it,—
I'm used to that.
But the least push of joy
Breaks up my feet,
And I tip—drunken.
Let no pebble smile,
'T was the new liquor,—
That was all!

Power is only pain,
Stranded, through discipline,
Till weights will hang.
Give balm to giants,
And they'll wilt, like men.
Give Himmaleh,—
They'll carry him!

X. *Escape*

I never hear the word "escape"
Without a quicker blood,
A sudden expectation,
A flying attitude.

I never hear of prisons broad
By soldiers battered down,
But I tug childish at my bars,—
Only to fail again!

XI. *Compensation*

For each ecstatic instant
We must an anguish pay
In keen and quivering ratio
To the ecstasy.

For each beloved hour
Sharp pittances of years,
Bitter contested farthings
And coffers heaped with tears.

XII. *The Martyrs*

Through the straight pass of suffering
The martyrs even trod,
Their feet upon temptation,
Their faces upon God.

A stately, shriven company;
Convulsion playing round,
Harmless as streaks of meteor
Upon a planet's bound.

Their faith the everlasting troth;
Their expectation fair;
The needle to the north degree
Wades so, through polar air.

XIII. *A Prayer*

I meant to have but modest needs,
Such as content, and heaven;
Within my income these could lie,
And life and I keep even.
But since the last included both,
It would suffice my prayer
But just for one to stipulate,
And grace would grant the pair.

And so, upon this wise I prayed,—
Great Spirit, give to me
A heaven not so large as yours,
But large enough for me.
A smile suffused Jehovah's face;
The cherubim withdrew;
Grave saints stole out to look at me,
And showed their dimples, too.

I left the place with all my might,—
My prayer away I threw;
The quiet ages picked it up,
And Judgment twinkled, too,
That one so honest be extant
As take the tale for true
That "Whatsoever you shall ask,
Itself be given you."

But I, grown shrewder, scan the skies
With a suspicious air,—
As children, swindled for the first,
All swindlers be, infer.

XIV

The thought beneath so slight a film
Is more distinctly seen,—
As laces just reveal the surge,
Or mists the Apennine.

XV

The soul unto itself
Is an imperial friend,—
Or the most agonizing spy
An enemy could send.

Secure against its own,
No treason it can fear;
Itself its sovereign, of itself
The soul should stand in awe.

XVI

Surgeons must be very careful
When they take the knife!
Underneath their fine incisions
Stirs the culprit,—Life!

XVII. *The Railway Train*

I like to see it lap the miles,
And lick the valleys up,
And stop to feed itself at tanks;
And then, prodigious, step

Around a pile of mountains,
And, supercilious, peer
In shanties by the sides of roads;
And then a quarry pare

To fit its sides, and crawl between,
Complaining all the while
In horrid, hooting stanza;
Then chase itself down hill

And neigh like Boanerges;
Then, punctual as a star,
Stop—docile and omnipotent—
At its own stable door.

XVIII. *The Show*

The show is not the show,
But they that go.
Menagerie to me
My neighbor be.
Fair play—
Both went to see.

XIX

Delight becomes pictorial
When viewed through pain,—
More fair, because impossible
That any gain.

The mountain at a given distance
In amber lies;
Approached, the amber flits a little,—
And that's the skies!

XX

A thought went up my mind to-day
That I have had before,
But did not finish,—some way back,
I could not fix the year,

Nor where it went, nor why it came
The second time to me,
Nor definitely what it was,
Have I the art to say.

But somewhere in my soul, I know
I've met the thing before;
It just reminded me—'t was all—
And came my way no more.

XXI

Is Heaven a physician?
   They say that He can heal;
But medicine posthumous
   Is unavailable.

Is Heaven an exchequer?
   They speak of what we owe;
But that negotiation
   I'm not a party to.

XXII. *The Return*

Though I get home how late, how late!
So I get home, 't will compensate.
Better will be the ecstasy
That they have done expecting me,
When, night descending, dumb and dark,
They hear my unexpected knock.
Transporting must the moment be,
Brewed from decades of agony!

To think just how the fire will burn,
Just how long-cheated eyes will turn
To wonder what myself will say,
And what itself will say to me,
Beguiles the centuries of way!

XXIII

A poor torn heart, a tattered heart,
That sat it down to rest,
Nor noticed that the ebbing day
Flowed silver to the west,
Nor noticed night did soft descend
Nor constellation burn,
Intent upon the vision
Of latitudes unknown.

The angels, happening that way,
This dusty heart espied;
Tenderly took it up from toil
And carried it to God.
There,—sandals for the barefoot;
There,—gathered from the gales,
Do the blue havens by the hand
Lead the wandering sails.

XXIV. *Too Much*

I should have been too glad, I see,
Too lifted for the scant degree
   Of life's penurious round;
My little circuit would have shamed
This new circumference, have blamed
   The homelier time behind.

I should have been too saved, I see,
Too rescued; fear too dim to me
   That I could spell the prayer
I knew so perfect yesterday,—
That scalding one, "Sabachthani,"
   Recited fluent here.

Earth would have been too much, I see,
And heaven not enough for me;
   I should have had the joy
Without the fear to justify,—
The palm without the Calvary;
   So, Saviour, crucify.

Defeat whets victory, they say;
The reefs in old Gethsemane
   Endear the shore beyond.
'T is beggars banquets best define;
'T is thirsting vitalizes wine,—
   Faith faints to understand.

XXV. *Shipwreck*

It tossed and tossed,—
A little brig I knew,—
O'ertook by blast,
It spun and spun,
And groped delirious, for morn.

It slipped and slipped,
As one that drunken stepped;
Its white foot tripped,
Then dropped from sight.

Ah, brig, good-night
To crew and you;
The ocean's heart too smooth, too blue,
To break for you.

XXVI

Experiment to me
Is every one I meet.
If it contain a kernel?
The figure of a nut

Presents upon a tree,
Equally plausibly;
But meat within is requisite,
To squirrels and to me.

XXVII

Victory comes late,
And is held low to freezing lips
Too rapt with frost
To take it.
How sweet it would have tasted,
Just a drop!
Was God so economical?
His table's spread too high for us
Unless we dine on tip-toe.
Crumbs fit such little mouths,
Cherries suit robins;
The eagle's golden breakfast
Strangles them.
God keeps his oath to sparrows,
Who of little love
Know how to starve!

XXVIII. *My Country's Wardrobe*

My country need not change her gown,
Her triple suit as sweet
As when 't was cut at Lexington,
And first pronounced "a fit."

Great Britain disapproves "the stars;"
Disparagement discreet,—
There's something in their attitude
That taunts her bayonet.

XXIX. *Enough*

God gave a loaf to every bird,
But just a crumb to me;
I dare not eat it, though I starve,—
My poignant luxury
To own it, touch it, prove the feat
That made the pellet mine,—
Too happy in my sparrow chance
For ampler coveting.

It might be famine all around,
I could not miss an ear,
Such plenty smiles upon my board,
My garner shows so fair.
I wonder how the rich may feel,—
An Indiaman—an Earl?
I deem that I with but a crumb
Am sovereign of them all.

XXX

Faith is a fine invention
For gentlemen who see;
But microscopes are prudent
In an emergency!

XXXI

Except the heaven had come so near,
So seemed to choose my door,
The distance would not haunt me so;
I had not hoped before.

But just to hear the grace depart
I never thought to see,
Afflicts me with a double loss;
'T is lost, and lost to me.

XXXII

Portraits are to daily faces
As an evening west
To a fine, pedantic sunshine
In a satin vest.

XXXIII. *The Duel*

I took my power in my hand
And went against the world;
'T was not so much as David had,
But I was twice as bold.

I aimed my pebble, but myself
Was all the one that fell.
Was it Goliath was too large,
Or only I too small?

XXXIV

A shady friend for torrid days
Is easier to find
Than one of higher temperature
For frigid hour of mind.

The vane a little to the east
Scares muslin souls away;
If broadcloth breasts are firmer
Than those of organdy,

Who is to blame? The weaver?
Ah! the bewildering thread!
The tapestries of paradise
So notelessly are made!

XXXV. *The Goal*

Each life converges to some centre
Expressed or still;
Exists in every human nature
A goal,

Admitted scarcely to itself, it may be,
Too fair
For credibility's temerity
To dare.

Adored with caution, as a brittle heaven,
To reach
Were hopeless as the rainbow's raiment
To touch,

Yet persevered toward, surer for the distance;
How high
Unto the saints' slow diligence
The sky!

Ungained, it may be, by a life's low venture,
But then,
Eternity enables the endeavoring
Again.

XXXVI. *Sight*

Before I got my eye put out,
I liked as well to see
As other creatures that have eyes,
And know no other way.

But were it told to me, to-day,
That I might have the sky
For mine, I tell you that my heart
Would split, for size of me.

The meadows mine, the mountains mine,—
All forests, stintless stars,
As much of noon as I could take
Between my finite eyes.

The motions of the dipping birds,
The lightning's jointed road,
For mine to look at when I liked,—
The news would strike me dead!

So, safer, guess, with just my soul
Upon the window-pane
Where other creatures put their eyes,
Incautious of the sun.

XXXVII

Talk with prudence to a beggar
Of 'Potosi' and the mines!
Reverently to the hungry
Of your viands and your wines!

Cautious, hint to any captive
You have passed enfranchised feet!
Anecdotes of air in dungeons
Have sometimes proved deadly sweet!

XXXVIII. *The Preacher*

He preached upon "breadth" till it argued him narrow,—
The broad are too broad to define;
And of "truth" until it proclaimed him a liar,—
The truth never flaunted a sign.

Simplicity fled from his counterfeit presence
As gold the pyrites would shun.
What confusion would cover the innocent Jesus
To meet so enabled a man!

XXXIX

Good night! which put the candle out?
A jealous zephyr, not a doubt.
　Ah! friend, you little knew
How long at that celestial wick
The angels labored diligent;
　Extinguished, now, for you!

It might have been the lighthouse spark
Some sailor, rowing in the dark,
　Had importuned to see!
It might have been the waning lamp
That lit the drummer from the camp
　To purer reveille!

XL

When I hoped I feared,
Since I hoped I dared;
Everywhere alone
As a church remain;
Spectre cannot harm,
Serpent cannot charm;
He deposes doom,
Who hath suffered him.

XLI. *Deed*

A deed knocks first at thought,
And then it knocks at will.
That is the manufacturing spot,
And will at home and well.

It then goes out an act,
Or is entombed so still
That only to the ear of God
Its doom is audible.

XLII. *Time's Lesson*

Mine enemy is growing old,—
I have at last revenge.
The palate of the hate departs;
If any would avenge,—

Let him be quick, the viand flits,
It is a faded meat.
Anger as soon as fed is dead;
'T is starving makes it fat.

XLIII. *Remorse*

Remorse is memory awake,
Her companies astir,—
A presence of departed acts
At window and at door.

It's past set down before the soul,
And lighted with a match,
Perusal to facilitate
Of its condensed despatch.

Remorse is cureless,—the disease
Not even God can heal;
For 't is his institution,—
The complement of hell.

XLIV. *The Shelter*

The body grows outside,—
The more convenient way,—
That if the spirit like to hide,
Its temple stands alway

Ajar, secure, inviting;
It never did betray
The soul that asked its shelter
In timid honesty.

XLV

Undue significance a starving man attaches
To food
Far off; he sighs, and therefore hopeless,
And therefore good.

Partaken, it relieves indeed, but proves us
That spices fly
In the receipt. It was the distance
Was savory.

XLVI

I many times thought peace had come,
When peace was far away;
As wrecked men deem they sight the land
At centre of the sea,

And struggle slacker, but to prove,
As hopelessly as I,
How many the fictitious shores
Before the harbor lie.

XLVII

Heart not so heavy as mine,
Wending late home,
As it passed my window
Whistled itself a tune,—

A careless snatch, a ballad,
A ditty of the street;
Yet to my irritated ear
An anodyne so sweet,

It was as if a bobolink,
Sauntering this way,
Carolled and mused and carolled,
Then bubbled slow away.

It was as if a chirping brook
Upon a toilsome way
Set bleeding feet to minuets
Without the knowing why.

To-morrow, night will come again,
Weary, perhaps, and sore.
Ah, bugle, by my window,
I pray you stroll once more!

XLVIII

Unto my books so good to turn
Far ends of tired days;
It half endears the abstinence,
And pain is missed in praise.

As flavors cheer retarded guests
With banquetings to be,
So spices stimulate the time
Till my small library.

It may be wilderness without,
Far feet of failing men,
But holiday excludes the night,
And it is bells within.

I thank these kinsmen of the shelf;
Their countenances bland
Enamour in prospective,
And satisfy, obtained.

XLIX

This merit hath the worst,—
It cannot be again.
When Fate hath taunted last
And thrown her furthest stone,

The maimed may pause and breathe,
And glance securely round.
The deer invites no longer
Than it eludes the hound.

L. *Prayer*

Prayer is the little implement
Through which men reach
Where presence is denied them.
They fling their speech

By means of it in God's ear;
If then He hear,
This sums the apparatus
Comprised in prayer.

LI. *Hunger*

I had been hungry all the years;
My noon had come, to dine;
I, trembling, drew the table near,
And touched the curious wine.

'T was this on tables I had seen,
When turning, hungry, lone,
I looked in windows, for the wealth
I could not hope to own.

I did not know the ample bread,
'T was so unlike the crumb
The birds and I had often shared
In Nature's dining-room.

The plenty hurt me, 't was so new,—
Myself felt ill and odd,
As berry of a mountain bush
Transplanted to the road.

Nor was I hungry; so I found
That hunger was a way
Of persons outside windows,
The entering takes away.

LII

I gained it so,
By climbing slow,
By catching at the twigs that grow
Between the bliss and me.
It hung so high,
As well the sky
Attempt by strategy.

I said I gained it,—
This was all.
Look, how I clutch it,
Lest it fall,
And I a pauper go;
Unfitted by an instant's grace
For the contented beggar's face
I wore an hour ago.

LIII

To learn the transport by the pain,
As blind men learn the sun;
To die of thirst, suspecting
That brooks in meadows run;

To stay the homesick, homesick feet
Upon a foreign shore
Haunted by native lands, the while,
And blue, beloved air—

This is the sovereign anguish,
This, the signal woe!
These are the patient laureates
Whose voices, trained below,

Ascend in ceaseless carol,
Inaudible, indeed,
To us, the duller scholars
Of the mysterious bard!

LIV. *Returning*

I years had been from home,
And now, before the door,
I dared not open, lest a face
I never saw before

Stare vacant into mine
And ask my business there.
My business,—just a life I left,
Was such still dwelling there?

I fumbled at my nerve,
I scanned the windows near;
The silence like an ocean rolled,
And broke against my ear.

I laughed a wooden laugh
That I could fear a door,
Who danger and the dead had faced,
But never quaked before.

I fitted to the latch
My hand, with trembling care,
Lest back the awful door should spring,
And leave me standing there.

I moved my fingers off
As cautiously as glass,
And held my ears, and like a thief
Fled gasping from the house.

LV

I know that he exists
Somewhere, in silence.
He has hid his rare life
From our gross eyes.

'T is an instant's play,
'T is a fond ambush,
Just to make bliss
Earn her own surprise!

But should the play
Prove piercing earnest,
Should the glee glaze
In death's stiff stare,

Would not the fun
Look too expensive?
Would not the jest
Have crawled too far?

LVI. *Melodies Unheard*

Musicians wrestle everywhere:
All day, among the crowded air,
   I hear the silver strife;
And—waking long before the dawn—
Such transport breaks upon the town
   I think it that "new life!"

It is not bird, it has no nest;
Nor band, in brass and scarlet dressed,
   Nor tambourine, nor man;
It is not hymn from pulpit read,—
The morning stars the treble led
   On time's first afternoon!

Some say it is the spheres at play!
Some say that bright majority
   Of vanished dames and men!
Some think it service in the place
Where we, with late, celestial face,
   Please God, shall ascertain!

LVII. *Called Back*

Just lost when I was saved!
Just felt the world go by!
Just girt me for the onset with eternity,
When breath blew back,
And on the other side
I heard recede the disappointed tide!

Therefore, as one returned, I feel,
Odd secrets of the line to tell!
Some sailor, skirting foreign shores,
Some pale reporter from the awful doors
Before the seal!

Next time, to stay!
Next time, the things to see
By ear unheard,
Unscrutinized by eye.

Next time, to tarry,
While the ages steal,—
Slow tramp the centuries,
And the cycles wheel.

Poems, Second Series: LOVE

I. *Choice*

Of all the souls that stand create
I have elected one.
When sense from spirit files away,
And subterfuge is done;

When that which is and that which was
Apart, intrinsic, stand,
And this brief tragedy of flesh
Is shifted like a sand;

When figures show their royal front
And mists are carved away,—
Behold the atom I preferred
To all the lists of clay!

II

I have no life but this,
To lead it here;
Nor any death, but lest
Dispelled from there;

Nor tie to earths to come,
Nor action new,
Except through this extent,
The realm of you.

III

Your riches taught me poverty.
Myself a millionnaire
In little wealths,—as girls could boast,—
Till broad as Buenos Ayre,

You drifted your dominions
A different Peru;
And I esteemed all poverty,
For life's estate with you.

Of mines I little know, myself,
But just the names of gems,—
The colors of the commonest;
And scarce of diadems

So much that, did I meet the queen,
Her glory I should know:
But this must be a different wealth,
To miss it beggars so.

I'm sure 't is India all day
To those who look on you
Without a stint, without a blame,—
Might I but be the Jew!

I'm sure it is Golconda,
Beyond my power to deem,—
To have a smile for mine each day,
How better than a gem!

At least, it solaces to know
That there exists a gold,
Although I prove it just in time
Its distance to behold!

It's far, far treasure to surmise,
And estimate the pearl
That slipped my simple fingers through
While just a girl at school!

IV. *The Contract*

I gave myself to him,
And took himself for pay.
The solemn contract of a life
Was ratified this way.

The wealth might disappoint,
Myself a poorer prove
Than this great purchaser suspect,
The daily own of Love

Depreciate the vision;
But, till the merchant buy,
Still fable, in the isles of spice,
The subtle cargoes lie.

At least, 't is mutual risk,—
Some found it mutual gain;
Sweet debt of Life,—each night to owe,
Insolvent, every noon.

V. *The Letter*

"Going to him! Happy letter! Tell him—
Tell him the page I didn't write;
Tell him I only said the syntax,
And left the verb and the pronoun out.
Tell him just how the fingers hurried,
Then how they waded, slow, slow, slow;
And then you wished you had eyes in your pages,
So you could see what moved them so.

"Tell him it wasn't a practised writer,
You guessed, from the way the sentence toiled;
You could hear the bodice tug, behind you,
As if it held but the might of a child;
You almost pitied it, you, it worked so.
Tell him—No, you may quibble there,
For it would split his heart to know it,
And then you and I were silenter.

"Tell him night finished before we finished,
And the old clock kept neighing 'day!'
And you got sleepy and begged to be ended—
What could it hinder so, to say?
Tell him just how she sealed you, cautious,
But if he ask where you are hid
Until to-morrow,—happy letter!
Gesture, coquette, and shake your head!"

VI

The way I read a letter 's this:
'T is first I lock the door,
And push it with my fingers next,
For transport it be sure.

And then I go the furthest off
To counteract a knock;
Then draw my little letter forth
And softly pick its lock.

Then, glancing narrow at the wall,
And narrow at the floor,
For firm conviction of a mouse
Not exorcised before,

Peruse how infinite I am
To—no one that you know!
And sigh for lack of heaven,—but not
The heaven the creeds bestow.

VII

Wild nights! Wild nights!
Were I with thee,
Wild nights should be
Our luxury!

Futile the winds
To a heart in port,—
Done with the compass,
Done with the chart.

Rowing in Eden!
Ah! the sea!
Might I but moor
To-night in thee!

VIII. *Possession*

Did the harebell loose her girdle
To the lover bee,
Would the bee the harebell hallow
Much as formerly?

Did the paradise, persuaded,
Yield her moat of pearl,
Would the Eden be an Eden,
Or the earl an earl?

IX. *At Home*

The night was wide, and furnished scant
With but a single star,
That often as a cloud it met
Blew out itself for fear.

The wind pursued the little bush,
And drove away the leaves
November left; then clambered up
And fretted in the eaves.

No squirrel went abroad;
A dog's belated feet
Like intermittent plush were heard
Adown the empty street.

To feel if blinds be fast,
And closer to the fire
Her little rocking-chair to draw,
And shiver for the poor,

The housewife's gentle task.
"How pleasanter," said she
Unto the sofa opposite,
"The sleet than May—no thee!"

X

A charm invests a face
Imperfectly beheld,—
The lady dare not lift her veil
For fear it be dispelled.

But peers beyond her mesh,
And wishes, and denies,—
Lest interview annul a want
That image satisfies.

XI

The moon is distant from the sea,
And yet with amber hands
She leads him, docile as a boy,
Along appointed sands.

He never misses a degree;
Obedient to her eye,
He comes just so far toward the town,
Just so far goes away.

Oh, Signor, thine the amber hand,
And mine the distant sea,—
Obedient to the least command
Thine eyes impose on me.

XII. *The Lovers*

The rose did caper on her cheek,
Her bodice rose and fell,
Her pretty speech, like drunken men,
Did stagger pitiful.

Her fingers fumbled at her work,—
Her needle would not go;
What ailed so smart a little maid
It puzzled me to know,

Till opposite I spied a cheek
That bore another rose;
Just opposite, another speech
That like the drunkard goes;

A vest that, like the bodice, danced
To the immortal tune,—
Till those two troubled little clocks
Ticked softly into one.

XIII

In lands I never saw, they say,
Immortal Alps look down,
Whose bonnets touch the firmament,
Whose sandals touch the town,—

Meek at whose everlasting feet
A myriad daisies play.
Which, sir, are you, and which am I,
Upon an August day?

XIV

He put the belt around my life,—
I heard the buckle snap,
And turned away, imperial,
My lifetime folding up
Deliberate, as a duke would do
A kingdom's title-deed,—
Henceforth a dedicated sort,
A member of the cloud.

Yet not too far to come at call,
And do the little toils
That make the circuit of the rest,
And deal occasional smiles
To lives that stoop to notice mine
And kindly ask it in,—
Whose invitation, knew you not
For whom I must decline?

XV. *The Lost Jewel*

I held a jewel in my fingers
And went to sleep.
The day was warm, and winds were prosy;
I said: " 'T will keep."

I woke and chid my honest fingers,—
The gem was gone;
And now an amethyst remembrance
Is all I own.

XVI

What if I say I shall not wait?
What if I burst the fleshly gate
And pass, escaped, to thee?
What if I file this mortal off,
See where it hurt me,—that's enough,—
And wade in liberty?

They cannot take us any more,—
Dungeons may call, and guns implore;
Unmeaning now, to me,
As laughter was an hour ago,
Or laces, or a travelling show,
Or who died yesterday!

Poems, Second Series: N A T U R E

I. *Mother Nature*

Nature, the gentlest mother,
Impatient of no child,
The feeblest or the waywardest,—
Her admonition mild

In forest and the hill
By traveller is heard,
Restraining rampant squirrel
Or too impetuous bird.

How fair her conversation,
A summer afternoon,—
Her household, her assembly;
And when the sun goes down

Her voice among the aisles
Incites the timid prayer
Of the minutest cricket,
The most unworthy flower.

When all the children sleep
She turns as long away
As will suffice to light her lamps;
Then, bending from the sky

With infinite affection
And infiniter care,
Her golden finger on her lip,
Wills silence everywhere.

II. *Out of the Morning*

Will there really be a morning?
Is there such a thing as day?
Could I see it from the mountains
If I were as tall as they?

Has it feet like water-lilies?
Has it feathers like a bird?
Is it brought from famous countries
Of which I have never heard?

Oh, some scholar! Oh, some sailor!
Oh, some wise man from the skies!
Please to tell a little pilgrim
Where the place called morning lies!

III

At half-past three a single bird
Unto a silent sky
Propounded but a single term
Of cautious melody.

At half-past four, experiment
Had subjugated test,
And lo! her silver principle
Supplanted all the rest.

At half-past seven, element
Nor implement was seen,
And place was where the presence was,
Circumference between.

IV. *Day's Parlor*

The day came slow, till five o'clock,
Then sprang before the hills
Like hindered rubies, or the light
A sudden musket spills.

The purple could not keep the east,
The sunrise shook from fold,
Like breadths of topaz, packed a night,
The lady just unrolled.

The happy winds their timbrels took;
The birds, in docile rows,
Arranged themselves around their prince
(The wind is prince of those).

The orchard sparkled like a Jew,—
How mighty 't was, to stay
A guest in this stupendous place,
The parlor of the day!

V. *The Sun's Wooing*

The sun just touched the morning;
The morning, happy thing,
Supposed that he had come to dwell,
And life would be all spring.

She felt herself supremer,—
A raised, ethereal thing;
Henceforth for her what holiday!
Meanwhile, her wheeling king

Trailed slow along the orchards
His haughty, spangled hems,
Leaving a new necessity,—
The want of diadems!

The morning fluttered, staggered,
Felt feebly for her crown,—
Her unanointed forehead
Henceforth her only one.

VI. *The Robin*

The robin is the one
That interrupts the morn
With hurried, few, express reports
When March is scarcely on.

The robin is the one
That overflows the noon
With her cherubic quantity,
An April but begun.

The robin is the one
That speechless from her nest
Submits that home and certainty
And sanctity are best.

VII. *The Butterfly's Day*

From cocoon forth a butterfly
As lady from her door
Emerged—a summer afternoon—
Repairing everywhere,

Without design, that I could trace,
Except to stray abroad
On miscellaneous enterprise
The clovers understood.

Her pretty parasol was seen
Contracting in a field
Where men made hay, then struggling hard
With an opposing cloud,

Where parties, phantom as herself,
To Nowhere seemed to go
In purposeless circumference,
As 't were a tropic show.

And notwithstanding bee that worked,
And flower that zealous blew,
This audience of idleness
Disdained them, from the sky,

Till sundown crept, a steady tide,
And men that made the hay,
And afternoon, and butterfly,
Extinguished in its sea.

VIII. *The Bluebird*

Before you thought of spring,
Except as a surmise,
You see, God bless his suddenness,
A fellow in the skies
Of independent hues,
A little weather-worn,
Inspiriting habiliments
Of indigo and brown.

With specimens of song,
As if for you to choose,
Discretion in the interval,
With gay delays he goes
To some superior tree
Without a single leaf,
And shouts for joy to nobody
But his seraphic self!

IX. *April*

An altered look about the hills;
A Tyrian light the village fills;
A wider sunrise in the dawn;
A deeper twilight on the lawn;
A print of a vermilion foot;
A purple finger on the slope;
A flippant fly upon the pane;
A spider at his trade again;
An added strut in chanticleer;
A flower expected everywhere;
An axe shrill singing in the woods;
Fern-odors on untravelled roads,—
All this, and more I cannot tell,
A furtive look you know as well,
And Nicodemus' mystery
Receives its annual reply.

X. *The Sleeping Flowers*

"Whose are the little beds," I asked,
"Which in the valleys lie?"
Some shook their heads, and others smiled,
And no one made reply.
"Perhaps they did not hear," I said;
"I will inquire again.
Whose are the beds, the tiny beds
So thick upon the plain?"
" 'T is daisy in the shortest;
A little farther on,
Nearest the door to wake the first,
Little leontodon.
" 'T is iris, sir, and aster,
Anemone and bell,
Batschia in the blanket red,
And chubby daffodil."
Meanwhile at many cradles
Her busy foot she plied,
Humming the quaintest lullaby
That ever rocked a child.
"Hush! Epigea wakens!
The crocus stirs her lids,
Rhodora's cheek is crimson,—
She's dreaming of the woods."
Then, turning from them, reverent,
"Their bed-time 't is," she said;
"The bumble-bees will wake them
When April woods are red."

XI. *My Rose*

Pigmy seraphs gone astray,
Velvet people from Vevay,
Belles from some lost summer day,
Bees' exclusive coterie.
Paris could not lay the fold
Belted down with emerald;
Venice could not show a cheek
Of a tint so lustrous meek.
Never such an ambuscade
As of brier and leaf displayed
For my little damask maid.
I had rather wear her grace
Than an earl's distinguished face;
I had rather dwell like her
Than be Duke of Exeter.
Royalty enough for me
To subdue the bumble-bee!

XII. *The Oriole's Secret*

To hear an oriole sing
May be a common thing,
Or only a divine.

It is not of the bird
Who sings the same, unheard.
As unto crowd.

The fashion of the ear
Attireth that it hear
In dun or fair.

So whether it be rune,
Or whether it be none,
Is of within;

The "tune is in the tree,"
The sceptic showeth me;
"No, sir! In thee!"

XIII. *The Oriole*

One of the ones that Midas touched,
Who failed to touch us all,
Was that confiding prodigal,
The blissful oriole.
So drunk, he disavows it
With badinage divine;
So dazzling, we mistake him
For an alighting mine.
A pleader, a dissembler,
An epicure, a thief,—
Betimes an oratorio,
An ecstasy in chief;
The Jesuit of orchards,
He cheats as he enchants
Of an entire attar
For his decamping wants.
The splendor of a Burmah,
The meteor of birds,
Departing like a pageant
Of ballads and of bards.
I never thought that Jason sought
For any golden fleece;
But then I am a rural man,
With thoughts that make for peace.
But if there were a Jason,
Tradition suffer me
Behold his lost emolument
Upon the apple-tree.

XIV. *In Shadow*

I dreaded that first robin so,
But he is mastered now,
And I'm accustomed to him grown,—
He hurts a little, though.
I thought if I could only live
Till that first shout got by,
Not all pianos in the woods
Had power to mangle me.
I dared not meet the daffodils,
For fear their yellow gown
Would pierce me with a fashion
So foreign to my own.
I wished the grass would hurry,
So when 't was time to see,
He'd be too tall, the tallest one
Could stretch to look at me.
I could not bear the bees should come,
I wished they'd stay away
In those dim countries where they go:
What word had they for me?
They're here, though; not a creature failed,
No blossom stayed away
In gentle deference to me,
The Queen of Calvary.
Each one salutes me as he goes,
And I my childish plumes
Lift, in bereaved acknowledgment
Of their unthinking drums.

XV. *The Humming-Bird*

A route of evanescence
With a revolving wheel;
A resonance of emerald,
A rush of cochineal;
And every blossom on the bush
Adjusts its tumbled head,—
The mail from Tunis, probably,
An easy morning's ride.

XVI. *Secrets*

The skies can't keep their secret!
They tell it to the hills—
The hills just tell the orchards—
And they the daffodils!

A bird, by chance, that goes that way
Soft overheard the whole.
If I should bribe the little bird,
Who knows but she would tell?

I think I won't, however,
It's finer not to know;
If summer were an axiom,
What sorcery had snow?

So keep your secret, Father!
I would not, if I could,
Know what the sapphire fellows do,
In your new-fashioned world!

XVII

Who robbed the woods,
The trusting woods?
The unsuspecting trees
Brought out their burrs and mosses
His fantasy to please.
He scanned their trinkets, curious,
He grasped, he bore away.
What will the solemn hemlock,
What will the fir-tree say?

XVIII. *Two Voyagers*

Two butterflies went out at noon
And waltzed above a stream,
Then stepped straight through the firmament
And rested on a beam;

And then together bore away
Upon a shining sea,—
Though never yet, in any port,
Their coming mentioned be.

If spoken by the distant bird,
If met in ether sea
By frigate or by merchantman,
Report was not to me.

XIX. *By the Sea*

I started early, took my dog,
And visited the sea;
The mermaids in the basement
Came out to look at me,

And frigates in the upper floor
Extended hempen hands,
Presuming me to be a mouse
Aground, upon the sands.

But no man moved me till the tide
Went past my simple shoe,
And past my apron and my belt,
And past my bodice too,

And made as he would eat me up
As wholly as a dew
Upon a dandelion's sleeve—
And then I started too.

And he—he followed close behind;
I felt his silver heel
Upon my ankle,—then my shoes
Would overflow with pearl.

Until we met the solid town,
No man he seemed to know;
And bowing with a mighty look
At me, the sea withdrew.

XX. *Old-Fashioned*

Arcturus is his other name,—
I'd rather call him star!
It's so unkind of science
To go and interfere!
I pull a flower from the woods,—
A monster with a glass
Computes the stamens in a breath,
And has her in a class.
Whereas I took the butterfly
Aforetime in my hat,
He sits erect in cabinets,
The clover-bells forgot.
What once was heaven, is zenith now.
Where I proposed to go
When time's brief masquerade was done,
Is mapped, and charted too!
What if the poles should frisk about
And stand upon their heads!
I hope I'm ready for the worst,
Whatever prank betides!
Perhaps the kingdom of Heaven's changed!
I hope the children there
Won't be new-fashioned when I come,
And laugh at me, and stare!
I hope the father in the skies
Will lift his little girl,—
Old-fashioned, naughty, everything,—
Over the stile of pearl!

XXI. *A Tempest*

An awful tempest mashed the air,
The clouds were gaunt and few;
A black, as of a spectre's cloak,
Hid heaven and earth from view.

The creatures chuckled on the roofs
And whistled in the air,
And shook their fists and gnashed their teeth,
And swung their frenzied hair.

The morning lit, the birds arose;
The monster's faded eyes
Turned slowly to his native coast,
And peace was Paradise!

XXII. *The Sea*

An everywhere of silver,
With ropes of sand
To keep it from effacing
The track called land.

XXIII. *In the Garden*

A bird came down the walk:
He did not know I saw;
He bit an angle-worm in halves
And ate the fellow, raw.

And then he drank a dew
From a convenient grass,
And then hopped sidewise to the wall
To let a beetle pass.

He glanced with rapid eyes
That hurried all abroad,—
They looked like frightened beads, I thought;
He stirred his velvet head

Like one in danger; cautious,
I offered him a crumb,
And he unrolled his feathers
And rowed him softer home

Than oars divide the ocean,
Too silver for a seam,
Or butterflies, off banks of noon,
Leap, plashless, as they swim.

XXIV. *The Snake*

A narrow fellow in the grass
Occasionally rides;
You may have met him,—did you not,
His notice sudden is.

The grass divides as with a comb,
A spotted shaft is seen;
And then it closes at your feet
And opens further on.

He likes a boggy acre,
A floor too cool for corn.
Yet when a child, and barefoot,
I more than once, at morn,

Have passed, I thought, a whip-lash
Unbraiding in the sun,—
When, stooping to secure it,
It wrinkled, and was gone.

Several of nature's people
I know, and they know me;
I feel for them a transport
Of cordiality;

But never met this fellow,
Attended or alone,
Without a tighter breathing,
And zero at the bone.

XXV. *The Mushroom*

The mushroom is the elf of plants,
At evening it is not;
At morning in a truffled hut
It stops upon a spot

As if it tarried always;
And yet its whole career
Is shorter than a snake's delay,
And fleeter than a tare.

'T is vegetation's juggler,
The germ of alibi;
Doth like a bubble antedate,
And like a bubble hie.

I feel as if the grass were pleased
To have it intermit;
The surreptitious scion
Of summer's circumspect.

Had nature any outcast face,
Could she a son contemn,
Had nature an Iscariot,
That mushroom,—it is him.

XXVI. *The Storm*

There came a wind like a bugle;
It quivered through the grass,
And a green chill upon the heat
So ominous did pass
We barred the windows and the doors
As from an emerald ghost;
The doom's electric moccasin
That very instant passed.
On a strange mob of panting trees,
And fences fled away,
And rivers where the houses ran
The living looked that day.
The bell within the steeple wild
The flying tidings whirled.
How much can come
And much can go,
And yet abide the world!

XXVII. *The Spider*

A spider sewed at night
Without a light
Upon an arc of white.
If ruff it was of dame
Or shroud of gnome,
Himself, himself inform.
Of immortality
His strategy
Was physiognomy.

XXVIII

I know a place where summer strives
With such a practised frost,
She each year leads her daisies back,
Recording briefly, "Lost."

But when the south wind stirs the pools
And struggles in the lanes,
Her heart misgives her for her vow,
And she pours soft refrains

Into the lap of adamant,
And spices, and the dew,
That stiffens quietly to quartz,
Upon her amber shoe.

XXIX

The one that could repeat the summer day
Were greater than itself, though he
Minutest of mankind might be.
And who could reproduce the sun,
At period of going down—
The lingering and the stain, I mean—
When Orient has been outgrown,
And Occident becomes unknown,
His name remain.

XXX

Nature rarer uses yellow
    Than another hue;
Saves she all of that for sunsets,—
    Prodigal of blue,

Spending scarlet like a woman,
    Yellow she affords
Only scantly and selectly,
    Like a lover's words.

XXXI. *The Wind's Visit*

The wind tapped like a tired man,
And like a host, "Come in,"
I boldly answered; entered then
My residence within

A rapid, footless guest,
To offer whom a chair
Were as impossible as hand
A sofa to the air.

No bone had he to bind him,
His speech was like the push
Of numerous humming-birds at once
From a superior bush.

His countenance a billow,
His fingers, if he pass,
Let go a music, as of tunes
Blown tremulous in glass.

He visited, still flitting;
Then, like a timid man,
Again he tapped—'t was flurriedly—
And I became alone.

XXXII. *Gossip*

The leaves, like women, interchange
   Sagacious confidence;
Somewhat of nods, and somewhat of
   Portentous inference,

The parties in both cases
   Enjoying secrecy,—
Inviolable compact
   To notoriety.

XXXIII. *Simplicity*

How happy is the little stone
That rambles in the road alone,
And doesn't care about careers,
And exigencies never fears;
Whose coat of elemental brown
A passing universe put on;
And independent as the sun,
Associates or glows alone,
Fulfilling absolute decree
In casual simplicity.

XXXIV. *Storm*

It sounded as if the streets were running,
And then the streets stood still.
Eclipse was all we could see at the window,
And awe was all we could feel.

By and by the boldest stole out of his covert,
To see if time was there.
Nature was in her beryl apron,
Mixing fresher air.

XXXV. *The Rat*

The rat is the concisest tenant.
He pays no rent,—
Repudiates the obligation,
On schemes intent.

Balking our wit
To sound or circumvent,
Hate cannot harm
A foe so reticent.

Neither decree
Prohibits him,
Lawful as
Equilibrium.

XXXVI

Frequently the woods are pink,
Frequently are brown;
Frequently the hills undress
Behind my native town.

Oft a head is crested
I was wont to see,
And as oft a cranny
Where it used to be.

And the earth, they tell me,
On its axis turned,—
Wonderful rotation
By but twelve performed!

XXXVII

Like mighty footlights burned the red
At bases of the trees,—
The far theatricals of day
Exhibiting to these.

'T was universe that did applaud
While, chiefest of the crowd,
Enabled by his royal dress,
Myself distinguished God.

XXXVIII. *A Thunder-Storm*

The wind begun to rock the grass
With threatening tunes and low,—
He flung a menace at the earth,
A menace at the sky.

The leaves unhooked themselves from trees
And started all abroad;
The dust did scoop itself like hands
And throw away the road.

The wagons quickened on the streets,
The thunder hurried slow;
The lightning showed a yellow beak,
And then a livid claw.

The birds put up the bars to nests,
The cattle fled to barns;
There came one drop of giant rain,
And then, as if the hands

That held the dams had parted hold,
The waters wrecked the sky,
But overlooked my father's house,
Just quartering a tree.

XXXIX. *With Flowers*

South winds jostle them,
Bumblebees come,
Hover, hesitate,
Drink, and are gone.

Butterflies pause
On their passage Cashmere;
I, softly plucking,
Present them here!

XL. *Fringed Gentian*

God made a little gentian;
It tried to be a rose
And failed, and all the summer laughed.
But just before the snows
There came a purple creature
That ravished all the hill;
And summer hid her forehead,
And mockery was still.
The frosts were her condition;
The Tyrian would not come
Until the North evoked it.
"Creator! shall I bloom?"

XLI. *Sunset*

Where ships of purple gently toss
On seas of daffodil,
Fantastic sailors mingle,
And then—the wharf is still.

XLII

She sweeps with many-colored brooms,
And leaves the shreds behind;
Oh, housewife in the evening west,
Come back, and dust the pond!

You dropped a purple ravelling in,
You dropped an amber thread;
And now you've littered all the East
With duds of emerald!

And still she plies her spotted brooms,
And still the aprons fly,
Till brooms fade softly into stars—
And then I come away.

XLIII. *Problems*

Bring me the sunset in a cup,
Reckon the morning's flagons up,
    And say how many dew;
Tell me how far the morning leaps,
Tell me what time the weaver sleeps
    Who spun the breadths of blue!

Write me how many notes there be
In the new robin's ecstasy
    Among astonished boughs;
How many trips the tortoise makes,
How many cups the bee partakes,—
    The debauchee of dews!

Also, who laid the rainbow's piers,
Also, who leads the docile spheres
    By withes of supple blue?
Whose fingers string the stalactite,
Who counts the wampum of the night,
    To see that none is due?

Who built this little Alban house
And shut the windows down so close
    My spirit cannot see?
Who'll let me out some gala day,
With implements to fly away,
    Passing pomposity?

XLIV. *The Juggler of Day*

Blazing in gold and quenching in purple,
Leaping like leopards to the sky,
Then at the feet of the old horizon
Laying her spotted face, to die;

Stooping as low as the otter's window,
Touching the roof and tinting the barn,
Kissing her bonnet to the meadow,—
And the juggler of day is gone!

XLV

It can't be summer,—that got through;
It's early yet for spring;
There's that long town of white to cross
Before the blackbirds sing.

It can't be dying,—it's too rouge,—
The dead shall go in white.
So sunset shuts my question down
With clasps of chrysolite.

XLVI. *My Cricket*

Farther in summer than the birds,
Pathetic from the grass,
A minor nation celebrates
Its unobtrusive mass.

No ordinance is seen,
So gradual the grace,
A pensive custom it becomes,
Enlarging loneliness.

Antiquest felt at noon
When August, burning low,
Calls forth this spectral canticle,
Repose to typify.

Remit as yet no grace,
No furrow on the glow,
Yet a druidic difference
Enhances nature now.

XLVII

As imperceptibly as grief
The summer lapsed away,—
Too imperceptible, at last,
To seem like perfidy.

A quietness distilled,
As twilight long begun,
Or Nature, spending with herself
Sequestered afternoon.

The dusk drew earlier in,
The morning foreign shone,—
A courteous, yet harrowing grace,
As guest who would be gone.

And thus, without a wing,
Or service of a keel,
Our summer made her light escape
Into the beautiful.

XLVIII. *Summer's Obsequies*

The gentian weaves her fringes,
The maple's loom is red.
My departing blossoms
Obviate parade.

A brief, but patient illness,
An hour to prepare;
And one, below this morning,
Is where the angels are.

It was a short procession,—
The bobolink was there,
An aged bee addressed us,
And then we knelt in prayer.

We trust that she was willing.—
We ask that we may be.
Summer, sister, seraph,
Let us go with thee!

In the name of the bee
And of the butterfly
And of the breeze, amen!

XLIX. *November*

Besides the autumn poets sing,
A few prosaic days
A little this side of the snow
And that side of the haze.

A few incisive mornings,
A few ascetic eves,—
Gone Mr. Bryant's golden-rod,
And Mr. Thomson's sheaves.

Still is the bustle in the brook,
Sealed are the spicy valves;
Mesmeric fingers softly touch
The eyes of many elves.

Perhaps a squirrel may remain,
My sentiments to share.
Grant me, O Lord, a sunny mind,
Thy windy will to bear!

L. *The Snow*

It sifts from leaden sieves,
It powders all the wood,
It fills with alabaster wool
The wrinkles of the road.

It makes an even face
Of mountain and of plain,—
Unbroken forehead from the east
Unto the east again.

It reaches to the fence,
It wraps it, rail by rail,
Till it is lost in fleeces;
It flings a crystal veil

On stump and stack and stem,—
The summer's empty room,
Acres of seams where harvests were,
Recordless, but for them.

It ruffles wrists of posts,
As ankles of a queen,—
Then stills its artisans like ghosts,
Denying they have been.

LI. *The Blue Jay*

No brigadier throughout the year
So civic as the jay.
A neighbor and a warrior too,
With shrill felicity

Pursuing winds that censure us
A February day,
The brother of the universe
Was never blown away.

The snow and he are intimate;
I've often seen them play
When heaven looked upon us all
With such severity,

I felt apology were due
To an insulted sky,
Whose pompous frown was nutriment
To their temerity.

The pillow of this daring head
Is pungent evergreens;
His larder—terse and militant—
Unknown, refreshing things;

His character a tonic,
His future a dispute;
Unfair an immortality
That leaves this neighbor out.

Poems, Second Series: TIME AND ETERNITY

I

Going to heaven!
I don't know when,
Pray do not ask me how,—
Indeed, I'm too astonished
To think of answering you!
Going to heaven!—
How dim it sounds!
And yet it will be done
As sure as flocks go home at night
Unto the shepherd's arm!

Perhaps you're going too!
Who knows?
If you should get there first,
Save just a little place for me
Close to the two I lost!
The smallest "robe" will fit me,
And just a bit of "crown;"
For you know we do not mind our dress
When we are going home.

I'm glad I don't believe it,
For it would stop my breath,
And I'd like to look a little more
At such a curious earth!
I am glad they did believe it
Whom I have never found
Since the mighty autumn afternoon
I left them in the ground.

II

Let down the bars, O Death!
The tired flocks come in
Whose bleating ceases to repeat,
Whose wandering is done.

Thine is the stillest night,
Thine the securest fold;
Too near thou art for seeking thee,
Too tender to be told.

III

At least to pray is left, is left.
O Jesus! in the air
I know not which thy chamber is,—
I'm knocking everywhere.

Thou stirrest earthquake in the South,
And maelstrom in the sea;
Say, Jesus Christ of Nazareth,
Hast thou no arm for me?

IV. *Epitaph*

Step lightly on this narrow spot!
The broadest land that grows
Is not so ample as the breast
These emerald seams enclose.

Step lofty; for this name is told
As far as cannon dwell,
Or flag subsist, or fame export
Her deathless syllable.

V

Morns like these we parted;
Noons like these she rose,
Fluttering first, then firmer,
To her fair repose.

Never did she lisp it,
And 't was not for me;
She was mute from transport,
I, from agony!

Till the evening, nearing,
One the shutters drew—
Quick! a sharper rustling!
And this linnet flew!

VI

A death-blow is a life-blow to some
Who, till they died, did not alive become;
Who, had they lived, had died, but when
They died, vitality begun.

VII

I read my sentence steadily,
Reviewed it with my eyes,
To see that I made no mistake
In its extremest clause,—

The date, and manner of the shame;
And then the pious form
That "God have mercy" on the soul
The jury voted him.

I made my soul familiar
With her extremity,
That at the last it should not be
A novel agony,

But she and Death, acquainted,
Meet tranquilly as friends,
Salute and pass without a hint—
And there the matter ends.

VIII

I have not told my garden yet,
Lest that should conquer me;
I have not quite the strength now
To break it to the bee.

I will not name it in the street,
For shops would stare, that I,
So shy, so very ignorant,
Should have the face to die.

The hillsides must not know it,
Where I have rambled so,
Nor tell the loving forests
The day that I shall go,

Nor lisp it at the table,
Nor heedless by the way
Hint that within the riddle
One will walk to-day!

IX. *The Battle-Field*

They dropped like flakes, they dropped like stars,
   Like petals from a rose,
When suddenly across the June
   A wind with fingers goes.

They perished in the seamless grass,—
   No eye could find the place;
But God on his repealless list
   Can summon every face.

X

The only ghost I ever saw
Was dressed in mechlin,—so;
He wore no sandal on his foot,
And stepped like flakes of snow.
His gait was soundless, like the bird,
But rapid, like the roe;
His fashions quaint, mosaic,
Or, haply, mistletoe.
His conversation seldom,
His laughter like the breeze
That dies away in dimples
Among the pensive trees.
Our interview was transient,—
Of me, himself was shy;
And God forbid I look behind
Since that appalling day!

XI

Some, too fragile for winter winds,
The thoughtful grave encloses,—
Tenderly tucking them in from frost
Before their feet are cold.

Never the treasures in her nest
The cautious grave exposes,
Building where schoolboy dare not look
And sportsman is not bold.

This covert have all the children
Early aged, and often cold,—
Sparrows unnoticed by the Father;
Lambs for whom time had not a fold.

XII

As by the dead we love to sit,
Become so wondrous dear,
As for the lost we grapple,
Though all the rest are here,—

In broken mathematics
We estimate our prize,
Vast, in its fading ratio,
To our penurious eyes!

XIII. *Memorials*

Death sets a thing significant
The eye had hurried by,
Except a perished creature
Entreat us tenderly

To ponder little workmanships
In crayon or in wool,
With "This was last her fingers did,"
Industrious until

The thimble weighed too heavy,
The stitches stopped themselves,
And then 't was put among the dust
Upon the closet shelves.

A book I have, a friend gave,
Whose pencil, here and there,
Had notched the place that pleased him,—
At rest his fingers are.

Now, when I read, I read not,
For interrupting tears
Obliterate the etchings
Too costly for repairs.

XIV

I went to heaven,—
'T was a small town,
Lit with a ruby,
Lathed with down.
Stiller than the fields
At the full dew,
Beautiful as pictures
No man drew.
People like the moth,
Of mechlin, frames,
Duties of gossamer,
And eider names.
Almost contented
I could be
'Mong such unique
Society.

XV

There is a shame of nobleness
Confronting sudden pelf,—
A finer shame of ecstasy
Convicted of itself.

A best disgrace a brave man feels,
Acknowledged of the brave,—
One more "Ye Blessed" to be told;
But this involves the grave.

XVI

Their height in heaven comforts not,
Their glory nought to me;
'T was best imperfect, as it was;
I'm finite, I can't see.

The house of supposition,
The glimmering frontier
That skirts the acres of perhaps,
To me shows insecure.

The wealth I had contented me;
If 't was a meaner size,
Then I had counted it until
It pleased my narrow eyes

Better than larger values,
However true their show;
This timid life of evidence
Keeps pleading, "I don't know."

XVII. *Triumph*

Triumph may be of several kinds.
There's triumph in the room
When that old imperator, Death,
By faith is overcome.

There's triumph of the finer mind
When truth, affronted long,
Advances calm to her supreme,
Her God her only throng.

A triumph when temptation's bribe
Is slowly handed back,
One eye upon the heaven renounced
And one upon the rack.

Severer triumph, by himself
Experienced, who can pass
Acquitted from that naked bar,
Jehovah's countenance!

XVIII

Pompless no life can pass away;
    The lowliest career
To the same pageant wends its way
    As that exalted here.
How cordial is the mystery!
    The hospitable pall
A "this way" beckons spaciously,—
    A miracle for all!

XIX

I noticed people disappeared,
When but a little child,—
Supposed they visited remote,
Or settled regions wild.

Now know I they both visited
And settled regions wild,
But did because they died,—a fact
Withheld the little child!

XX. *Following*

I had no cause to be awake,
My best was gone to sleep,
And morn a new politeness took,
And failed to wake them up,

But called the others clear,
And passed their curtains by.
Sweet morning, when I over-sleep,
Knock, recollect, for me!

I looked at sunrise once,
And then I looked at them,
And wishfulness in me arose
For circumstance the same.

'T was such an ample peace,
It could not hold a sigh,—
'T was Sabbath with the bells divorced,
'T was sunset all the day.

So choosing but a gown
And taking but a prayer,
The only raiment I should need,
I struggled, and was there.

XXI

If anybody's friend be dead,
It's sharpest of the theme
The thinking how they walked alive,
At such and such a time.

Their costume, of a Sunday,
Some manner of the hair,—
A prank nobody knew but them,
Lost, in the sepulchre.

How warm they were on such a day:
You almost feel the date,
So short way off it seems; and now,
They're centuries from that.

How pleased they were at what you said;
You try to touch the smile,
And dip your fingers in the frost:
When was it, can you tell,

You asked the company to tea,
Acquaintance, just a few,
And chatted close with this grand thing
That don't remember you?

Past bows and invitations,
Past interview, and vow,
Past what ourselves can estimate,—
That makes the quick of woe!

XXII. *The Journey*

Our journey had advanced;
Our feet were almost come
To that odd fork in Being's road,
Eternity by term.

Our pace took sudden awe,
Our feet reluctant led.
Before were cities, but between,
The forest of the dead.

Retreat was out of hope,—
Behind, a sealed route,
Eternity's white flag before,
And God at every gate.

XXIII. *A Country Burial*

Ample make this bed.
Make this bed with awe;
In it wait till judgment break
Excellent and fair.

Be its mattress straight,
Be its pillow round;
Let no sunrise' yellow noise
Interrupt this ground.

XXIV. *Going*

On such a night, or such a night,
Would anybody care
If such a little figure
Slipped quiet from its chair,

So quiet, oh, how quiet!
That nobody might know
But that the little figure
Rocked softer, to and fro?

On such a dawn, or such a dawn,
Would anybody sigh
That such a little figure
Too sound asleep did lie

For chanticleer to wake it,—
Or stirring house below,
Or giddy bird in orchard,
Or early task to do?

There was a little figure plump
For every little knoll,
Busy needles, and spools of thread,
And trudging feet from school.

Playmates, and holidays, and nuts,
And visions vast and small.
Strange that the feet so precious charged
Should reach so small a goal!

XXV

Essential oils are wrung:
The attar from the rose
Is not expressed by suns alone,
It is the gift of screws.

The general rose decays;
But this, in lady's drawer,
Makes summer when the lady lies
In ceaseless rosemary.

XXVI

I lived on dread; to those who know
The stimulus there is
In danger, other impetus
Is numb and vital-less.

As 't were a spur upon the soul,
A fear will urge it where
To go without the spectre's aid
Were challenging despair.

XXVII

If I should die,
And you should live,
And time should gurgle on,
And morn should beam,
And noon should burn,
As it has usual done;
If birds should build as early,
And bees as bustling go,—
One might depart at option
From enterprise below!
'T is sweet to know that stocks will stand
When we with daisies lie,
That commerce will continue,
And trades as briskly fly.
It makes the parting tranquil
And keeps the soul serene,
That gentlemen so sprightly
Conduct the pleasing scene!

XXIX. *Ghosts*

One need not be a chamber to be haunted,
One need not be a house;
The brain has corridors surpassing
Material place.

Far safer, of a midnight meeting
External ghost,
Than an interior confronting
That whiter host.

Far safer through an Abbey gallop,
The stones achase,
Than, moonless, one's own self encounter
In lonesome place.

Ourself, behind ourself concealed,
Should startle most;
Assassin, hid in our apartment,
Be horror's least.

The prudent carries a revolver,
He bolts the door,
O'erlooking a superior spectre
More near.

XXVIII. *At Length*

Her final summer was it,
And yet we guessed it not;
If tenderer industriousness
Pervaded her, we thought

A further force of life
Developed from within,—
When Death lit all the shortness up,
And made the hurry plain.

We wondered at our blindness,—
When nothing was to see
But her Carrara guide-post,—
At our stupidity.

When, duller than our dulness,
The busy darling lay,
So busy was she, finishing,
So leisurely were we!

XXX. *Vanished*

She died,—this was the way she died;
And when her breath was done,
Took up her simple wardrobe
And started for the sun.

Her little figure at the gate
The angels must have spied,
Since I could never find her
Upon the mortal side.

XXXI

What inn is this
Where for the night
Peculiar traveller comes?
Who is the landlord?
Where the maids?
Behold, what curious rooms!
No ruddy fires on the hearth,
No brimming tankards flow.
Necromancer, landlord,
Who are these below?

XXXII. *Gone*

Went up a year this evening!
I recollect it well!
Amid no bells nor bravos
The bystanders will tell!
Cheerful, as to the village,
Tranquil, as to repose,
Chastened, as to the chapel,
This humble tourist rose.
Did not talk of returning,
Alluded to no time
When, were the gales propitious,
We might look for him;
Was grateful for the roses
In life's diverse bouquet,
Talked softly of new species
To pick another day.
Beguiling thus the wonder,
The wondrous nearer drew;
Hands bustled at the moorings—
The crowd respectful grew.
Ascended from our vision
To countenances new!
A difference, a daisy,
Is all the rest I knew!

XXXIII. *Precedence*

Wait till the majesty of Death
Invests so mean a brow!
Almost a powdered footman
Might dare to touch it now!

Wait till in everlasting robes
This democrat is dressed,
Then prate about "preferment"
And "station" and the rest!

Around this quiet courtier
Obsequious angels wait!
Full royal is his retinue,
Full purple is his state!

A lord might dare to lift the hat
To such a modest clay,
Since that my Lord, "the Lord of lords"
Receives unblushingly!

XXXIV. *Requiem*

Taken from men this morning,
Carried by men to-day,
Met by the gods with banners
Who marshalled her away.

One little maid from playmates,
One little mind from school,—
There must be guests in Eden;
All the rooms are full.

Far as the east from even,
Dim as the border star,—
Courtiers quaint, in kingdoms,
Our departed are.

XXXV

A throe upon the features
A hurry in the breath,
An ecstasy of parting
Denominated "Death,"—

An anguish at the mention,
Which, when to patience grown,
I've known permission given
To rejoin its own.

XXXVI

It was not death, for I stood up,
And all the dead lie down;
It was not night, for all the bells
Put out their tongues, for noon.

It was not frost, for on my flesh
I felt siroccos crawl,—
Nor fire, for just my marble feet
Could keep a chancel cool.

And yet it tasted like them all;
The figures I have seen
Set orderly, for burial,
Reminded me of mine,

As if my life were shaven
And fitted to a frame,
And could not breathe without a key;
And 't was like midnight, some,

When everything that ticked has stopped
And space stares, all around,
Or grisly frosts, first autumn morns,
Repeal the beating ground.

But most like chaos,—stopless, cool,—
Without a chance or spar,
Or even a report of land
To justify despair.

XXXVII. *Till the End*

I should not dare to leave my friend,
Because—because if he should die
While I was gone, and I—too late—
Should reach the heart that wanted me;

If I should disappoint the eyes
That hunted, hunted so, to see,
And could not bear to shut until
They "noticed" me—they noticed me;

If I should stab the patient faith
So sure I'd come—so sure I'd come,
It listening, listening, went to sleep
Telling my tardy name,—

My heart would wish it broke before,
Since breaking then, since breaking then,
Were useless as next morning's sun,
Where midnight frosts had lain!

XXXVIII. *Void*

Great streets of silence led away
To neighborhoods of pause;
Here was no notice, no dissent,
No universe, no laws.

By clocks 't was morning, and for night
The bells at distance called;
But epoch had no basis here,
For period exhaled.

XXXIX. *The Forgotten Grave*

After a hundred years
Nobody knows the place,—
Agony, that enacted there,
Motionless as peace.

Weeds triumphant ranged,
Strangers strolled and spelled
At the lone orthography
Of the elder dead.

Winds of summer fields
Recollect the way,—
Instinct picking up the key
Dropped by memory.

XL. *Saved!*

Of tribulation these are they
Denoted by the white;
The spangled gowns, a lesser rank
Of victors designate.

All these did conquer; but the ones
Who overcame most times
Wear nothing commoner than snow,
No ornament but palms.

Surrender is a sort unknown
On this superior soil;
Defeat, an outgrown anguish,
Remembered as the mile

Our panting ankle barely gained
When night devoured the road;
But we stood whispering in the house,
And all we said was "Saved"!

XLI

I think just how my shape will rise
When I shall be forgiven,
Till hair and eyes and timid head
Are out of sight, in heaven.

I think just how my lips will weigh
With shapeless, quivering prayer
That you, so late, consider me,
The sparrow of your care.

I mind me that of anguish sent,
Some drifts were moved away
Before my simple bosom broke,—
And why not this, if they?

And so, until delirious borne
I con that thing,—"forgiven,"—
Till with long fright and longer trust
I drop my heart, unshriven!

XLII

Lay this laurel on the one
Too intrinsic for renown.
Laurel! veil your deathless tree,—
Him you chasten, that is he!

Selections from

POEMS: THIRD SERIES

The Editor's Commentary

Poems by Emily Dickinson: Third Series (1896) was edited and arranged wholly by Mabel Loomis Todd. Although the poet's best work had been supposedly winnowed and the choicest examples included in the two preceding volumes, the *Third Series* contained some of her most candid and startling lines.

Mrs. Todd's Preface was exceptionally brief. It consisted of only three paragraphs, none of which were more than just relevant. She wrote in part: "The intellectual activity of Emily Dickinson was so great that a large and characteristic choice is still possible among her literary material, and this third volume of her verses is put forth in response to the repeated wish of the admirers of her peculiar genius. . . . There is internal evidence that many of the poems were simply spontaneous flashes of insight, apparently unrelated to outward circumstance. . . . The surroundings in which any of Emily Dickinson's verses are known to have been written usually serve to explain them clearly; but in general the present volume is full of thoughts needing no interpretation to those who apprehend this scintillating spirit."

"Scintillating" is the word most often used by the commentators who first discovered Emily Dickinson. But it scarcely serves today. Beneath the kaleidoscopic sparkle there is a singing flame that leaps high, and, feeding the flame, there is a fire that is always intense though the burning is quiet.

§

Superiority to fate
  Is difficult to learn
'Tis not conferred by any,
  But possible to earn

A pittance at a time,
  Until, to her surprise,
The soul with strict economy
  Subsists till Paradise.

§

Forbidden fruit a flavor has
  That lawful orchards mocks;
How luscious lies the pea within
  The pod that Duty locks!

§

Could mortal lip divine
  The undeveloped freight
Of a delivered syllable,
  'Twould crumble with the weight.

The brain is wider than the sky,
   For, put them side by side,
The one the other will include
   With ease, and you beside.

The brain is deeper than the sea,
   For, hold them, blue to blue,
The one the other will absorb,
   As sponges, buckets do.

The brain is just the weight of God,
   For, lift them, pound for pound,
And they will differ, if they do,
   As syllable from sound.

A Word

A word is dead
   When it is said,
Some say.
   I say it just
Begins to live
   That day.

§

How still the bells in steeples stand,
   Till, swollen with the sky,
They leap upon their silver feet
   In frantic melody!

Parting

My life closed twice before its close;
   It yet remains to see
If Immortality unveil
   A third event to me,

So huge, so hopeless to conceive
   As these that twice befell.
Parting is all we know of heaven,
   And all we need of hell.

A Book

There is no frigate like a book
   To take us lands away,
Nor any coursers like a page
   Of prancing poetry.

This traverse may the poorest take
   Without oppress of toll.
How frugal is the chariot
   That bears a human soul!

The Lost Thought

I felt a cleavage in my mind
   As if my brain had split;
I tried to match it, seam by seam,
   But could not make them fit.

The thought behind I strove to join
   Unto the thought before,
But sequence ravelled out of reach
   Like balls upon a floor.

Disenchantment

It dropped so low in my regard
  I heard it hit the ground.
And go to pieces on the stones
  At bottom of my mind:

Yet blamed the fate that fractured, less
  Than I reviled myself
For entertaining plated wares
  Upon my silver shelf.

Desire

Who never wanted,—maddest joy
  Remains to him unknown;
The banquet of abstemiousness
  Surpasses that of wine.

Within its hope, though yet ungrasped
  Desire's perfect goal,
No nearer, lest reality
  Should disenthrall thy soul.

What soft, cherubic creatures
    These gentlewomen are!
One would as soon assault a plush
    Or violate a star!

Such dimity convictions,
    A horror so refined
Of freckled human nature,
    Of Deity ashamed,—

It's such a common glory,
    A fisherman's degree!
Redemption, brittle lady,
    Be so, ashamed of thee.

Longing

I envy seas whereon he rides,
  I envy spokes of wheels
Of chariots that him convey,
  I envy speechless hills

That gaze upon his journey;
  How easy all can see
What is forbidden utterly
  As heaven, unto me!

I envy nests of sparrows
  That dot his distant eaves,
The wealthy fly upon his pane,
  The happy, happy leaves

That just abroad his window
  Have summer's leave to be,
The earrings of Pizarro
  Could not obtain for me.

§

Love is anterior to life,
  Posterior to death,
Initial of creation, and
  The exponent of breath.

Loyalty

Split the lark and you'll find the music,
　　Bulb after bulb, in silver rolled,
Scantily dealt to the summer morning,
　　Saved for your ear when lutes be old.

Loose the flood, you shall find it patent,
　　Gush after gush, reserved for you;
Scarlet experiment! sceptic Thomas,
　　Now, do you doubt that your bird was true?

§

Heart, we will forget him!
　　You and I, to-night!
You may forget the warmth he gave,
　　I will forget the light.

When you have done, pray tell me,
　　That I my thoughts may dim.
Haste! lest while you're lagging,
　　I may remember him!

§

Father, I bring thee not myself,—
　　That were the little load;
I bring thee the imperial heart
　　I had not strength to hold.

The heart I cherished in my own
　　Till mine too heavy grew;
Yet strangest, heavier since it went,
　　Is it too large for you?

§

To make a prairie it takes a clover
    And one bee,—
One clover, and a bee,
And revery.
The revery alone will do
If bees are few.

§

Not knowing when the dawn will come
    I open every door;
Or has it feathers like a bird,
    Or billows like a shore?

§

The springtime's pallid landscape
　　Will glow like bright bouquet,
Though drifted deep in parian
　　The village lies to-day.

The lilacs, bending many a year,
　　With purple load will hang;
The bees will not forget the tune
　　Their old forefathers sang.

The rose will redden in the bog,
　　The aster on the hill
Her everlasting fashion set,
　　And covenant gentians frill,

Till summer folds her miracle
　　As women do their gown,
Or priests adjust the symbols
　　When sacrament is done.

The Waking Year

A lady red upon the hill
    Her annual secret keeps;
A lady white within the field
    In placid lily sleeps!

The tidy breezes with their brooms
    Sweep vale, and hill, and tree!
Prithee, my pretty housewives!
    Who may expected be?

The neighbors do not yet suspect!
    The woods exchange a smile—
Orchard, and buttercup, and bird—
    In such a little while!

And yet how still the landscape stands,
    How nonchalant the wood,
As if the resurrection
    Were nothing very odd!

§

They say that "time assuages,"—
　　Time never did assuage;
An actual suffering strengthens,
　　As sinews do, with age.

Time is a test of trouble,
　　But not a remedy.
If such it prove, it prove too
　　There was no malady.

§

This was in the white of the year,
　　That was in the green,
Drifts were as difficult then to think
　　As daisies now to be seen.

Looking back is best that is left,
　　Or if it be before,
Retrospection is prospect's half,
　　Sometimes almost more.

Immortality

It is an honorable thought,
    And makes one lift one's hat,
As one encountered gentlefolk
    Upon a daily street,

That we've immortal place,
    Though pyramids decay,
And kingdoms, like the orchard,
    Flit russetly away.

§

A toad can die of light!
    Death is the common right
Of toads and men,—
    Of earl and midge
The privilege.
    Why swagger then?
The gnat's supremacy
    Is large as thine.

§

I felt a funeral in my brain,
  And mourners, to and fro.
Kept treading, treading, till it seemed
  That sense was breaking through.

And when they all were seated,
  A service like a drum
Kept beating, beating, till I thought
  My mind was going numb.

And then I heard them lift a box,
  And creak across my soul
With those same boots of lead, again.
  Then space began to toll

As all the heavens were a bell,
  And Being but an ear,
And I and silence some strange race,
  Wrecked, solitary, here.

Dying

I heard a fly buzz when I died;
　　The stillness round my form
Was like the stillness in the air
　　Between the heaves of storm.

The eyes beside had wrung them dry,
　　And breaths were gathering sure
For that last onset, when the king
　　Be witnessed in his power.

I willed my keepsakes, signed away
　　What portion of me I
Could make assignable,—and then
　　There interposed a fly,

With blue, uncertain, stumbling buzz,
　　Between the light and me;
And then the windows failed, and then
　　I could not see to see.

§

There's been a death in the opposite house
   As lately as to-day.
I know it by the numb look
   Such houses have alway.

The neighbors rustle in and out,
   The doctor drives away.
A window opens like a pod,
   Abrupt, mechanically.

Somebody flings a mattress out,—
   The children hurry by;
They wonder if It died on that,—
   I used to when a boy.

The minister goes stiffly in
   As if the house were his,
And he owned all the mourners now,
   And little boys besides;

And then the milliner, and the man
   Of the appalling trade,
To take the measure of the house,
   There'll be that dark parade

Of tassels and of coaches soon;
   It's easy as a sign,—
The intuition of the news
   In just a country town.

Selections from

"THE SINGLE HOUND"

The Editor's Commentary

The Single Hound was the fourth selection of Emily Dickinson's poetry and the first to be made and edited by her niece, Martha Dickinson Bianchi. Twenty-eight years had passed between the publication of *Poems: Third Series* (1896) and *The Single Hound* (1914), but Mme. Bianchi made no effort to explain the lapse or account for the sudden appearance of more than one hundred and forty new poems. Daughter of Emily's brother, Austin, and his wife Sue, Mme. Bianchi had inherited the Dickinson estate and had discovered many "hidden documents" after the death of Lavinia. Her preface to the collection is personal and almost embarrassingly fatuous, but there are occasional glimpses which add substance to the Dickinson legend.

There is, for example, the paragraph describing Emily's reactions to the sexes. "She usually liked men better than women because they were more stimulating. I can see her yet, standing in the spacious upper hall a Summer afternoon, finger on lip, and hear her say, as the feminine callers took their departure— 'Listen! Hear them kiss, the traitors!' To most women she was a provoking puzzle. To her, in turn, most women were a form of triviality to be escaped when feasible. But stupidity had no sex with her, and I equally well remember her spying down upon a stranger sent to call upon her by a mutual friend, and dismissing him unreceived after one glance from her window, remarking— 'His face is as handsome and as meaningless as the full moon.' At another time she called me to peep at a new Professor recently come to the college saying: 'Look dear, he is pretty as a cloth Pink!' her mouth curling in derision as she uttered it and one hand motioning as if to throw the flower away."

Here the legend comes to life, and the poet is heard in the very accents which individualize her verse.

Adventure most unto itself
The Soul condemned to be;
Attended by a Single Hound—
Its own Identity.

§

Beauty crowds me till I die,
Beauty, mercy have on me!
But if I expire today,
Let it be in sight of thee.

§

The Soul's superior instants
Occur to Her alone,
When friend and earth's occasion
Have infinite withdrawn.

Or she, Herself, ascended
To too remote a height,
For lower recognition
Than Her Omnipotent.

This mortal abolition
Is seldom, but as fair
As apparition—subject
To autocratic air.

Eternity's disclosure
To favorites, a few,
Of the colossal substance
Of immortality.

§

Lightly stepped a yellow star
To its lofty place,
Loosed the Moon her silver hat
From her lustral face.
All of evening softly lit
As an astral hall—
"Father," I observed to Heaven,
"You are punctual."

§

Fame is a fickle food
Upon a shifting plate,
Whose table once a guest, but not
The second time, is set.
Whose crumbs the crows inspect,
And with ironic caw
Flap past it to the Farmer's corn;
Men eat of it and die.

This quiet Dust was Gentlemen and Ladies,
    And Lads and Girls;
Was laughter and ability and sighing,
    And frocks and curls.
This passive place a Summer's nimble mansion,
    Where Bloom and Bees
Fulfilled their Oriental Circuit,
    Then ceased like these.

§

"Heavenly Father," take to thee
The supreme iniquity,
Fashioned by thy candid hand
In a moment contraband.
Though to trust us seem to us
More respectful—"we are dust."
We apologize to Thee
For Thine own duplicity.

§

All circumstances are the frame
In which His Face is set,
All latitudes exist for His
Sufficient continent.

The light His action and the dark
The leisure of His Will,
In Him existence serve, or set
A force illegible.

Selections from

"FURTHER POEMS"

The Editor's Commentary

Further Poems of Emily Dickinson (1929) appeared in print fifteen years after *The Single Hound*. Like its predecessor, the volume was copyright by Martha Dickinson Bianchi, but Emily Dickinson's niece added the name of a friend, Alfred Leete Hampson, to her own as collaborative editor. To the title page she also added the tantalizing line: "Withheld from Publication by Her Sister Lavinia."

Nothing was divulged in Mme. Bianchi's rhapsodic and rambling introduction except three semi-evasive sentences: "When the little, unexplored package gave up these poems of Emily Dickinson which her sister, Lavinia, saw fit never to publish, it was for one breathless instant as if the bright apparition of Emily had returned to the old house, with the bees and the birds still busy beneath her window, to salute us with her wings. . . . It is possible that these were intended for another volume in the series already published. It is certain that to destroy them would be heresy to the faith of her following." This was a puzzling statement. It was hard to believe that Mme. Bianchi, who inherited and lived in the Dickinson home, never made a thorough search of the place. It was even more alarming to contemplate the thought that the poems were ever in danger of being "destroyed." It now seemed likely that these were the poems which Mabel Loomis Todd had selected to be the fourth volume in the series which she had previously edited, and had returned to Lavinia after the bitter quarrel between the two households. That the poems were lost or mislaid and finally recovered is possible, but it is unlikely that they were purposely withheld. In any case, the neglected manuscript became one more memento of the memory of Emily Dickinson and a renewed proof of her genius. Had she written nothing but this one book, she would have to be ranked among the poets whose lines are deathless. Small in bulk, fine in texture, here is the "colossal substance of immortality."

§

I reckon, when I count at all,
First Poets—then the Sun—
Then Summer—then the heaven of God—
And then the list is done.
But looking back—the first so seems
To comprehend the whole—
The others look a needless show,
So I write Poets—All.
This summer lasts a solid year,
They can afford a sun
The East would deem extravagant,
And if the final Heaven
Be beautiful as they disclose
To those who trust in them,
It is too difficult a grace
To justify the dream.

§

Experience is the angled road
Preferred against the mind
By paradox, the mind itself
Presuming it to lead
Quite opposite. How complicate
The discipline of man,
Compelling him to choose himself
His pre-appointed pain.

§

Forever is composed of Nows—
'Tis not a different time,
Except for infiniteness
And latitude of home.

From this, experienced here,
Remove the dates to these,
Let months dissolve in further months,
And years exhale in years.

Without certificate or pause
Or celebrated days,
As infinite our years would be
As Anno Domini's.

§

She dealt her pretty words like blades;
As glittering they shone,
And every one unbared a nerve
Or wantoned with a bone.

She never deemed she hurt;
That is not steel's affair.
A vulgar grimace in the flesh
How ill the creatures bear!

To ache is human, not polite;
The film upon the eye
Mortality's old custom—
Just locking up to die.

§

At leisure is the Soul
That gets a staggering blow;
The width of Life
Before it spreads
Without a thing to do.

It begs you give it work,
But just the placing pins—
Or humblest patchwork
Children do—
To help its vacant hands.

§

I've known a Heaven like a tent
To wrap its shining yards,
Pluck up its stakes and disappear
Without the sound of boards
Or rip of nail, or carpenter,
But just the miles of stare
That signalize a show's retreat
In North America.
No trace, no figment of the thing
That dazzled yesterday,
No ring, no marvel;
Men and feats
Dissolved as utterly
As birds' far navigation
Discloses just a hue;
A plash of oars—a gayety,
Then swallowed up to view.

§

Of course I prayed—
And did God care?
He cared as much as
On the air
A bird had stamped her foot
And cried "Give me!"

My reason, life
I had not had, but for
Yourself,
'Twere better charity
To leave me in the atom's
Tomb,
Merry and nought, and gay
And numb,
Than this smart misery.

§

The rainbow never tells me
That gust and storm are by;
Yet is she more convincing
Than philosophy.

My flowers turn from forums,
Yet eloquent declare
What Cato couldn't prove to me
Except the birds were here!

§

The mountains grow unnoticed,
Their purple figures rise
Without attempt, exhaustion,
Assistance or applause.

In their eternal faces
The sun with broad delight
Looks long—and last, and golden,
For fellowship at night.

§

The world feels dusty
When we stop to die;
We want the dew then,
Honors taste dry.

Flags vex a dying face,
But the least fan
Stirred by a friend's hand
Cools like the rain.

Mine be the ministry
When thy thirst comes,
Dews of thyself to fetch
And holy balms.

§

The only news I know
Is bulletins all day
From Immortality.

The only shows I see
To-morrow and To-day,
Perchance Eternity.

The only One I meet
Is God,—the only street
Existence, this traversed

If other news there be,
Or admirabler show—
I'll tell it you.

§

I took one draught of life,
I'll tell you what I paid,
Precisely an existence—
The market price, they said.

They weighed me, dust by dust,
They balanced film with film,
Then handed me my being's worth—
A single dram of Heaven.

§

It was a quiet way
He asked if I was his.
I made no answer of the tongue,
But answer of the eyes.

And then he bore me high
Before this mortal noise,
With swiftness as of chariots
And distance as of wheels.

The world did drop away
As countries from the feet
Of him that leaneth in balloon
Upon an ether street.

The gulf behind was not—
The continents were new.
Eternity it was—before
Eternity was due.

No seasons were to us;
It was not night nor noon;
For sunrise stopped upon the place
And fastened it in dawn.

§

After great pain a formal feeling comes—
The nerves sit ceremonious like tombs;
The stiff heart questions—was it he that bore?
And yesterday—or centuries before?

The feet mechanical go round
A wooden way
Of ground or air or Ought,
Regardless grown,
A quartz contentment like a stone.

This is the hour of lead
Remembered if outlived
As freezing persons recollect the snow—
First chill, then stupor, then
The letting go.

Postscript: The Editor's Commentary

Unpublished Poems of Emily Dickinson first appeared in a limited edition of 525 copies in 1935. It was, like the preceding volume, edited by Martha Dickinson Bianchi and Alfred Leete Hampson. It carried neither introduction nor any prefatory matter except a paragraph which informed the reader that the new verses were "disclosed during the exhaustive examination of the Dickinson family papers," and were "made obligatory by the increasing posthumous fame of the poet." No indication was given as to why or by whom these poems were withheld. Nor were all of the poems hitherto "unpublished." Some verses had appeared in the *Letters*; some had been part of longer poems previously printed. But even the slightest of them give fresh insights into the poet's renunciation, her inner drama, "manifold for anguish," and her heroism in defeat. Here, once more, is Emily Dickinson's peculiar vitality, which strikes, as F. O. Matthiessen wrote, "an exact balance between abstraction and sensation."

Bolts of Melody was published in 1945. Edited by Millicent Todd Bingham with the help of her mother, Mabel Loomis Todd (as detailed in The Editor's Introduction), the collection contained some 650 poems, scraps, and segments of unfinished poems, most of which had remained unpublished in any form. Although none of the verses surpassed those previously printed, the selections reaffirmed the strength and power of Emily Dickinson's seemingly fragile stanzas and proved that her importance, negligible at first, had become incalculable.

An Alphabetic Listing

OF THOSE POEMS WHICH HAVE TITLES

An Index

A toad can die of light! 245
A train went through a burial gate, **76**
A word is dead, 233
A wounded deer leaps highest, 11
    Beauty crowds me till I die, 252
Because I could not stop for Death, 88
Before I got my eye put out, 125
Before you thought of spring, 161
Belshazzar had a letter, 25
Besides the autumn poets sing, 192
Blazing in gold and quenching in purple, 188
Bring me the sunset in a cup, 187
    Come slowly, Eden! 42
Could mortal lip divine, 231
    Dare you see a soul at the white heat? 106
Death is a dialogue between, 91
Death sets a thing significant, 205
Delayed till she had ceased to know, 72
Delight becomes pictorial, 114
Departed to the judgment, 73
Did the harebell loose her girdle, 147
Doubt me, my dim companion! 31
    Each life converges to some centre, 124
Elysium is as far as to, 30
Essential oils are wrung, 214
Except the heaven had come so near, 122
Except to heaven, she is nought, 90
Experience is the angled road, 259
Experiment to me, 119
Exultation is the going, 75
    Faith is a fine invention, 121
Fame is a fickle food, 254
Farther in summer than the birds, 189
Father, I bring thee not myself, 240
Forbidden fruit a flavor has, 231
For each ecstatic instant, 109
Forever is composed of Nows, 261
Frequently the woods are pink, 183
From cocoon forth a butterfly, 160
    Glee! the great storm is over! 9
God gave a loaf to every bird, 121
God made a little gentian, 185
God permits industrious angels, 84
Going to heaven! 197